Copyright © 2023 by Troy Andrews

# Bridges and Barriers

## Practical Psychology for Persuasive Presentations

## Troy Andrews

PRESENTATIONPERSUASION.COM

# CONTENTS

# THE APPROACH

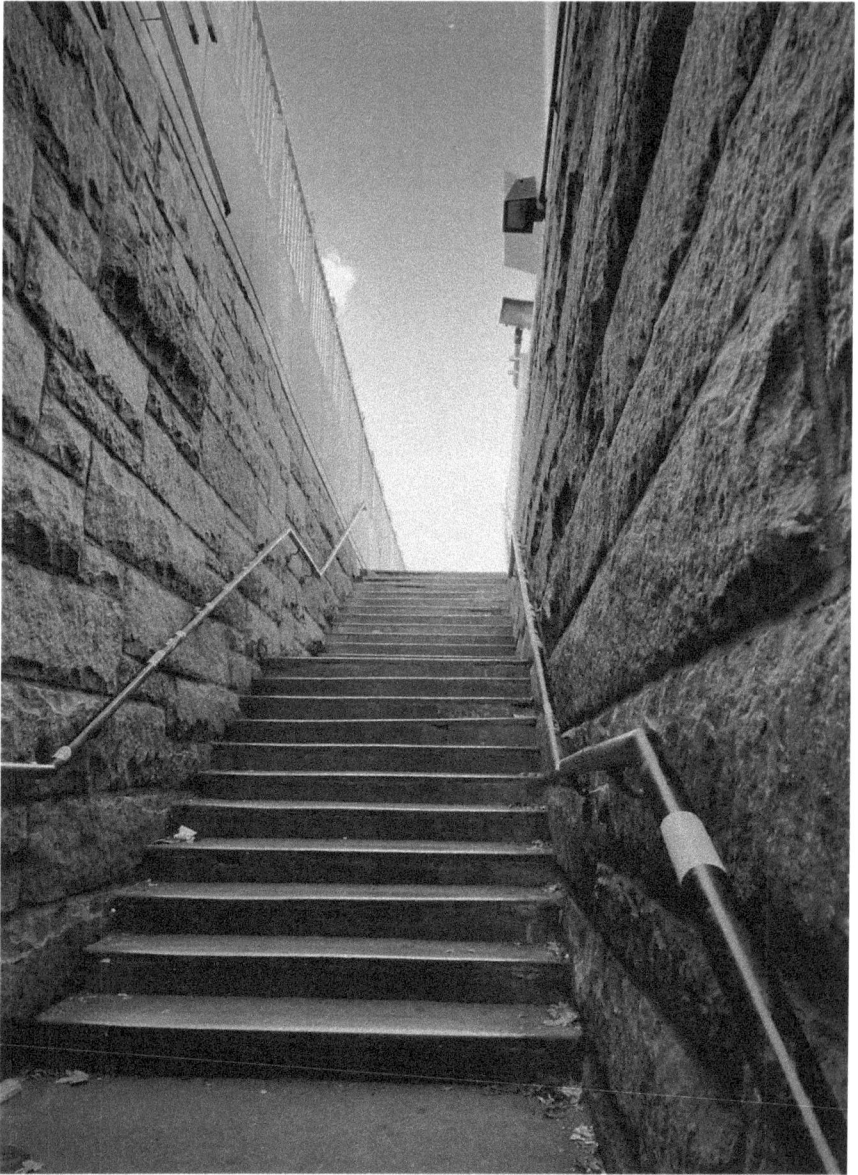

"A bridge is a meeting place... a possibility, a metaphor."

**Jeanette Winterson (poet)**

P RESENTATIONS ARE THE BRIDGES that carry your audience to Change. This is a book about change. It's based on the concept that every presentation should end in change for your audience. A change in knowledge, understanding, attitude, behavior, and even a change of mind.

How many times have you seen (or delivered) a presentation that had no impact, effect, or change? A data dump – an overloaded, overtime, and overwhelmingly boring presentation.

This book is committed to enabling and empowering you to optimize your messages for maximum impact. Through a clear methodology, useful case studies, examples, stories, and practical applications, you'll be ready to incorporate strategic and persuasive psychology in your very next presentation.

Imagine having true confidence in your presentations because you have a methodology to clearly identify your goals and design a persuasive strategy to reach them. No more fake it till you make it, believe it until you achieve it, or talk it till you walk it. No more imposter syndrome. Imagine how that confidence would feel.

I'm going to share with you a methodology that is efficient, effective, and effortless. OK, well it's definitely efficient and effective. Realistically, it's not effortless. Persuasion is definitely not easy. Changing minds is difficult. But with the tips, tricks, and techniques I give you in this book, you will soon be on your way to a future full of presentations optimized for persuasion. And yes, it will get easier with time.

I use bridges here as a metaphor for presentations, and I use the iconic Brooklyn Bridge as the prime example due to my affinity with it and the extraordinary story and rich history it holds. In this book I will relate stories about the Brooklyn Bridge to how you can design your next presentation. As I tell these historic stories, I'll draw practical parallels to persuasive presentations.

At the beginning of each section, I will tell a brief part of the origin story of the Brooklyn Bridge and those who were involved. After that, I'll share some similarities and parallels to modern presentations. Finally, I'll show the practical applications you can add to your own presentation strategy.

I have a personal relationship with the Brooklyn Bridge as I lived in New York for more than 16 years. For many years I lived in Brooklyn Heights on Orange Street in a third-floor walkup, in an old brownstone with a huge bay window, a mere few blocks from the stairs that lead up to the Bridge's walkway.

The Bridge connects modern-day Manhattan, where Wall Street meets Chinatown, to the Brooklyn side, landing between the historic brownstones of the Brooklyn Heights area and the recently upcycled DUMBO (Down Under Manhattan Bridge Overpass) neighborhood. This Bridge spans the river to join these disparate neighborhoods as thousands daily pass over by vehicle and on foot. Yet beneath them lies a story sunk deep down into the river. There is both a public and a personal story to tell.

# Presentations
## are the **Bridges**
## that carry your
# Audience
## to
# Change

The Bridge is approachable and offers a great user experience. It has a unique wooden walkway that is easy to walk, run, or bike on and offers a soft base compared to the concrete jungle that is the rest of the city.

I used to run it every day after work. It offers respite and sanctuary from the cars, traffic, and noise of the city. The wooden walkway is elevated so traffic flows below the walkway to the left and the right. It provides a great view of Brooklyn, Manhattan, the Statue of Liberty, and the river below.

Tourists from every reach of the world pour across in droves, eager to experience New York City by crossing the Bridge that they have seen in so many movies.

The Brooklyn Bridge is one of the most iconic landmarks in the world. It's approachable yet stately, romantic yet cold.

I'm slightly biased because I lived there for many years, which has personal significance. I feel like the Bridge truly has character, grit, and personality; yes, it has a story to tell.

The Brooklyn Bridge is also designed to make you feel good about crossing it. It's grandiose in size, evoking confidence, yet approachable and easily traversed, making it both trustworthy and user friendly.

W HEN WE GIVE A speech, a lecture, or a presentation, we are trying to take our audience somewhere: to discover a new place, have a new thought, experience a new feeling, behold a new idea, ponder a new concept, start a new behavior, take a new action – Change.

For some, change is exciting, for others, terrifying. In this book, we will cover how to design a presentation that will lead your audiences to cross the bridge to change.

I use bridges and the Brooklyn Bridge in particular here as a metaphor for both presentations and communication in general. The methodology in this book is unique in its simplicity.

I feel that bridges can convey people physically, emotionally, mentally, and even spiritually to new places.

I've been a presentation coach for more than 15 years now and I've analyzed and coached thousands of presenters over my career. I've dug deep into the details of what makes a good speech, and what makes people agree, align, and approve.

Although my methodology is quite simple, its execution will be a skill that you will continue to hone for the rest of your life. That being said, it is a skill you can practice, improve, and perfect with every presentation.

The persuasive techniques in this book are practical, principled, and psychological.

PRACTICAL: Easy to understand, remember, and apply.
PRINCIPLED: Positive, ethical, and fair. Mutually beneficial (win/win) and long-term relationship oriented.
PSYCHOLOGICAL: Based on Behavioral Science and Behavioral Economics principles.

These techniques are designed to work with the brain in a way that helps facilitate judgment and decision-making.

This book is NOT about manipulation, coercion, deception, or other "dark arts" of persuasion.

When you have finished this book, you will be able to design your presentations more quickly, effectively, and persuasively.

There are many books on public speaking skills. This is not one of them.

There are many books on basic business presentation design. This is not one of them.

This book is a practical guide to adding strategic and persuasive psychology to your presentations. It's unique because it is an Applied Behavioral Science and Behavioral Economics approach to persuasive presentations.

Behavioral Science is the study of judgment and decision-making. Behavioral Economics is very similar but leans more towards economic decisions.

In this book, I'll outline my A|B|C methodology, which I've created and used with my clients to simplify the design process of modern-day presentations. It's based on modern discoveries and insights from Neuroscience, Psychology, Persuasion Theory, Behavioral Science, Behavioral Economics, and the ancient, time-tested public speaking skills of traditional Rhetoric.

I created this methodology in response to the recurring need of my clients to strategically focus their presentations and craft a well-designed strategy to persuade. Time after time they struggle with having a clear goal and/or a way to get there.

This methodology applies to all forms of general communication, whether written or spoken. That means you will learn to write more persuasive emails, negotiate more effectively, have more meaningful conversations, make better sales pitches, etc.

I've been using this methodology for many years and have slowly refined it. I've also updated these principles with the latest understandings of the brain and cognition.

**Secrets of suasive strategy**

First of all, yes, suasive is a real word (same meaning as persuasive). Before becoming a presentation designer and coach, I was in the construction industry for more than 16 years in Brooklyn. I worked my way up from a common laborer to project management in charge of entire sites and the construction of multistory concrete structures in all five boroughs of New York City. My job was coordinating the many different aspects of the construction process. I had to work and coordinate with the architects and engineers, construction crews, regulatory agencies, inspectors, external vendors and suppliers, local police, neighbors and neighborhood committees of our projects – the list was endless.

Along that journey, I quickly learned that presenting myself and my message clearly and persuasively was key to building relationships, trust, and loyalty. I also saw that people communicate differently across different levels, places, situations, and times. When you add in the vast diversity of different personalities and backgrounds, it gets even more complicated.

I realized that communication needs to be focused, planned, and strategic.

At the same time I also became aware of the fields of Behavioral Science and Behavioral Economics.

In 2005 I came across the book *Freakonomics* by Stephen D. Levitt, an economist, and Stephen J. Dubner, his journalist writing partner. It dealt with how and why people make judgments, using data and numbers to decipher the mysteries of decision-making. This fascinated me because I saw that slight changes in approach, angle, and messaging often made the difference between success and failure. What if I could apply some of these ideas to my communication skills? Could I increase the persuasiveness of my messages?

In 2008 came the two books *Predictably Irrational,* by Dan Ariely, and *Nudge,* by Richard Thaler and Cass Sunstein. These two books really opened my eyes to the world of Behavioral Economics, a subset of both Behavioral Science and Traditional Economics.

*Predictably Irrational* showed that humans make decisions that aren't always based on logic, as traditional economic theories had previously implied. It pointed out the many ways that we are pulled into the ebb and flow of our emotions. Often by changing the packaging, angle, or delivery of the message, we can change others' decisions and judgments.

*Nudge* was yet another eye-opening book. Nudge Theory is about what the book calls "choice architecture," which is the deliberate sequencing or design of the environment, message, or choice itself to optimize preferable decisions. It is a vital part of Behavioral Economics and thus a good point of reference for the principles involved.

Probably the best and also my favorite example of applied Nudge Theory originated at Schiphol Airport in Amsterdam. The cleaning crews were struggling with a rather pervasive problem of "spillage" in front of the urinals in the men's bathrooms. Besides being utterly disgusting, it took a lot of extra work and vigilance to keep up with.

Signs appealing to civility and cleanliness pleaded with the users to pay more attention or move forward, all with no measurable results. (Side note: I live in Shanghai, China, and a common sign I see in front of the urinal says, "One small step for man, one giant leap for mankind," urging men to get a little closer to the urinal. I'm pretty sure Neil Armstrong never meant or imagined his words being used like that, but I digress.)

Finally, someone had an idea. An unconventional, almost bizarre idea that seemed to come from a drunken brainstorming session in an Amsterdam coffee shop. It would later prove to effectively reduce the problem and give some rare insight into the male brain.

They simply affixed a small sticker of a common housefly inside the urinal. This gave the incentive for the user to focus on a "target" and direct his aim. This succeeded in reducing "spillage" by over 70%!

This effect was clear and measurable. It required no persuasion, convincing facts, or emotional appeals to civility, cleanliness, or common decency. Although the target was visible to all participants, the psychological, influential factors were, in all respects, invisible.

Eureka! What if there was a way to apply that type of invisible psychology to our everyday and business communication and presentations?

**Behavior is your savior**

Nudge Theory involves setting up choices in such a way that the optimal choice is the path of least resistance, which becomes most desirable for the user. This makes it the obvious choice.

Sometimes people won't even know that they're making a decision at all. This can work for approvals, agreements, negotiations, changes in attitude, behavior, and sometimes opinions.

Yes, influence can be subtle and invisible, yet seductive and irresistible.

And that's the persuasive appeal of Behavioral Economics. We're talking about behavior, and behavior is often not rational. The reason people say they do things is often not the real reason. Behavioral Economics realizes that sometimes we choose or reject things emotionally and rationalize with logic afterward.

As famed investment banker J.P. Morgan once said, "A man always has two reasons for what he does – a good one, and the real one."

Behavioral Science and Behavioral Economics are both studies of judgment and decision-making. They are the study of how things are, not the way that so-called common sense would dictate they should be.

Behavioral Science explores the cognitive processes and the behavioral interactions between people. It includes Psychology, Anthropology, and Cognitive Science. Behavioral Science studies the effects of psychological, cognitive, emotional, cultural, and social factors on people's decisions.

Behavioral Science is a genre, and Behavioral Economics could be thought of as a sub-genre: a hybrid of psychology and economic theory. It eschews traditional fundamental concepts of economic theory – that people make purely rational and logical decisions based purely on fact.

For example, the traditional economic law of demand states that when the price of a product increases, demand will naturally fall, and conversely when the price decreases, demand will increase.

Yet consider for a moment the Veblen paradox. Veblen goods are items that become more desirable the more expensive they are. Think iPhone, or expensive luxury bags, shoes, and the like. Often we equate value with price so just by increasing the price of something, value is implied.

Behavioral Economics observes the decisions that people make and then unearths the underlying principles that drive our decisions. We can often see how other people make emotional decisions that go against logic and common sense. We naturally tend to think that this is only the folly of others. It's tough to think of ourselves that way, unfortunately.

Judgments and decisions are made up of part logic, part emotions. The ratio of each depends on many internal and external factors.

Our emotions often skew our opinions of ourselves and of others. We have different cognitive biases as well. These are mental filters that distort our view of reality. They can be false beliefs, prejudices, misunderstandings, or emotional preferences.

Consider one example, dubbed the Dunning-Kruger Effect. This bias is about how people with relatively low or average knowledge or skill often will overestimate their true abilities in relation to others.

For example, if someone asks you if you're a good driver, you're likely to say that you are not the best, but you are definitely above average. If we were to ask 100 people the same question and then tally up everyone's self-evaluation, we would quickly see that the vast majority would say they are above average. Statistically, that's impossible. Anecdotally, I once asked everyone in a large workshop to raise their hands if they felt they were an above average driver. Everyone raised their hands: 100% thought they were above average.

That's the result of just one bias. Now add in the hundreds of other biases at play, and we can quickly see that we are not as logical and rational as we like to think.

And yet, we are quick to say that we wouldn't want to be viewed as purely logical. Being viewed as or called a Spock from *Star Trek* wouldn't sit well. Conversely, we wouldn't want to be viewed as a Homer Simpson either, driven by base emotions, fears, and desires, would we?

So we reside somewhere in the middle. But that Homer Simpson part is still there. We are all subject to irrational thoughts, fears, and beliefs. These aspects shape the way we make decisions.

The insight that our emotions are connected to our decisions was noticed long ago.

"A man always has **2** Reasons for what he does **a good one,** and the

**real one.**

- J P Morgan

## Head like a hole

If you visit the Warren Anatomical Museum at Harvard University in Massachusetts, you'll find an intriguing specimen. There you will find a skull that belonged to a man named Phineas Gage.

Phineas worked for the railroads. In 1848, he was on a crew that cleared away large rocks as the track-laying crew approached. His job was to come behind the drillers and put dynamite in the hole. After that, he would put some sand in there and tamp it down with a heavy steel rod. One day as he was tamping it down, the steel rod sparked against a rock, causing the dynamite to explode.

The steel rod in his hand shot right through his skull, going through his neck and straight out the top of his head, slicing right through part of his brain. The rod landed several yards away. The steel rod was 43 inches (1.09 m) long and over an inch (2.54 cm) wide. It weighed more than 13 pounds (5.89 kgs)! Gruesome, I know, but bear with me.

Although he was instantly thrown to the ground, amazingly, Phineas stood up imme-diately after it happened.

He walked over to his supervisor to get help.
When the doctor arrived, he calmly explained what happened and
how he felt.

Phineas not only miraculously survived, he was mostly the same as
before his accident, except for being blind in one eye. His doctor
pronounced him fully recovered after a few months. One thing
was very different, though. Everyone that knew him before the
accident said he was no longer himself. He had all the knowledge
that he had before and could remember people and events. But
his personality and decision-making were not the same.

In 1868, his doctor, John Martyn Harlow, published a paper noting
his observations: "The equilibrium or balance, so to speak, between his intellectual faculties and animal propensities, seems to
have been destroyed. He is fitful, irreverent, indulging at times in
the grossest profanity (which was not previously his custom), man-
ifesting but little deference for his fellows, impatient of restraint
or advice when it conflicts with his desires, at times pertinaciously
obstinate, yet capricious and vacillating, devising many plans of
future operations, which are no sooner arranged than they are
abandoned in turn for others appearing more feasible. A child
in his intellectual capacity and manifestations, he has the animal
passions of a strong man."

"Previous to his injury, though untrained in the schools, he possessed a well-balanced mind, and was looked upon by those who
knew him as a shrewd, smart business man, very energetic and
persistent in executing all his plans of operation. In this regard
his mind was radically changed, so decidedly that his friends and
acquaintances said he was 'no longer Gage.'"

In a 1994 study, researchers reconstructed Gage's skull using a new neuroimaging technique. They wanted to find out precisely where he was injured. They found that he suffered injuries to his left and right prefrontal cortices. This would result in problems with both his emotional processing and rational decision-making. The lack of emotion meant a lack of decision-making ability. Emotions directly influence decision-making.

# The lack of **emotion** meant a lack of **Decision - making ability.**

A modern doctor has been studying this same phenomenon for many years. Neuroscientist Dr. Antonio Damasio worked with a few patients who had parts of their brains removed, particularly the part that processes emotions. He too noticed their inability to make decisions.

One patient would spend 30 minutes trying to choose a time for his next session with the doctor. Dr. Damasio would observe him and take notes. If the doctor didn't stop him, he could spend the day weighing the pros and cons of two different time slots. Yes, emotions are the drivers for decisions.

I'll throw in some anecdotal evidence as well. Working in the corporate world, dealing with many different types of companies, I get to work with many top tier decision-makers.

One day, one of the executives of a large Fortune 500 E-commerce company told me he had asked the CFO of the company what percentage of all C-suite decisions he felt were emotionally driven. 10%, 50%, 80%? His answer? He told him it was more like 90%. Yes, even at the executive level, the majority make decisions based on gut feelings.

In a recent study by Price Waterhouse Cooper and written by the Economist Intelligence Unit, senior leaders in the UK were asked how they made major decisions. 30% said by their intuition and experience, 31% said by the experience of others, and 29% cited data and analytics. That's profound when you think about it.

Decisions are often influenced by our gut feelings. These are a mix of past experience and knowledge, as well as our ego, core desires, what mood we are in, the time of day, how it will make us look, etc.

Once we accept this fact, we can start to look at our judgments and decisions differently and more objectively.

Moreover, we can also start observing how others form judgments and decisions. We can then find ways to use that knowledge and insight to help persuade and influence others.

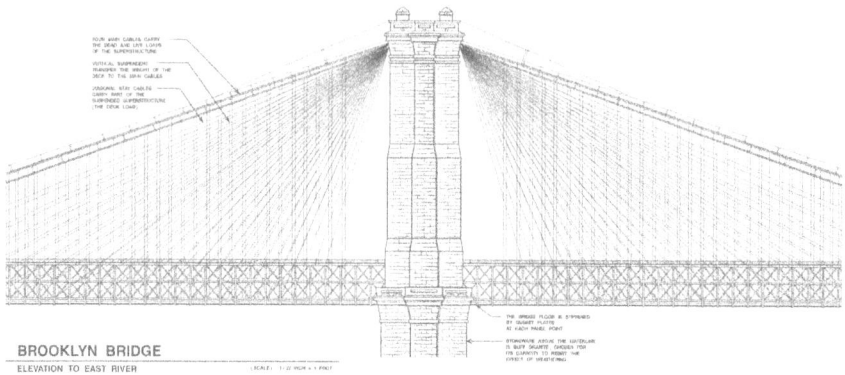

BROOKLYN BRIDGE
ELEVATION TO EAST RIVER

## Intelligent design

Bridges are designed. Design means that there are many considerations to keep in mind. All these aspects lead to trust in the planning, the process, and the product.

There are the *reputational* aspects of the designers' credibility and that of the construction team.
There are the *engineering* aspects of the structure successfully and safely carrying a load.
There are the *psychological* aspects that give the user a feeling of safety and confidence. Design considerations of how something looks and feels can inspire trust.

Presentations are also designed. There are the *reputational* aspects of the presenter: their experience, credentials, and knowledge. There are the *engineering* aspects of the logic, proof, and evidence that form a foundation to carry and support the message. There are the *psychological* aspects of moving an audience and making them feel safe, comfortable, and trusting – how the message looks, feels, and is perceived.

More than 2,000 years ago, Aristotle wrote *On Rhetoric,* a book focused on persuasive speeches. He spoke of 3 main aspects that every persuasive speech needs: an appeal to Ethos, Logos, and

Pathos.

ETHOS = Credibility: Competence, confidence, and credentials. We need to know we can trust the person.
LOGOS = Logic: Facts, figures, and findings. We need to know we can trust the evidence.
PATHOS = Emotion: Drive, desire, and devotion. We need to be motivated and open to change.

You can probably see the parallel to the bridge analogy.

Reputation - Ethos
Engineering - Logos
Psychology - Pathos

All three are needed. I find most people focus on logic and credibility, but forget the psychological aspects of emotion.

Most of my presentation coaching clients come to me primarily expecting public speaking skills. They want to speak in a style that is charming, charismatic, and confident. Indeed it's a good goal to come across as articulate and eloquent. These are all skills that can be learned, honed, and arguably perfected. These skills bear a close kinship with those of acting and improv. Most desire to have an effortless onstage confidence.

But If you just focus on your public speaking skills, and your content has no substance, you might hear some colleagues say "good job," yet you still might walk away wondering why you didn't get the approval, alignment, or agreement you wanted.

I see very few presenters focusing on the psychological persuasiveness of their message. A successful presentation doesn't just end with a pat on the back and a "job well done." It ends with the audience leaving differently than they came in: changed.

Bolstering charisma and eloquence can help you build up a form of confidence. But the best way to boost true confidence is to truly believe in the message you are communicating and have a clear strategy to hit your target.

Otherwise, you become the ubiquitous salesperson who can sell anything to anybody, yet often leaves clients with buyer's regret because they bought into the act, but not the message. This isn't a farsighted strategy and is not what ethical business is about. The accurate measure of a presentation's effectiveness is its success at changing your audience.

You want trust, mutual respect, and a spirit of collaboration that ends with both parties getting what they need and desire. You want your audiences coming back for more business in the future.

If you are to step onto a bridge, you want to have the utmost confidence in the ability of that bridge to carry your weight. In a presentation, your audience must trust that the destination is what they want and that the bridge will safely carry them across.

Your bridge, your presentation, needs to be engineered to evoke trust by logically and emotionally carrying your audience across to change. You're taking your audience on a journey. And to cross that bridge, they will need to trust you and your content, and feel good about the destination.

OK, so now that I've explained the background and concepts behind my methodology, let me introduce you to the process!

**The A|B|C persuasive presentation methodology**

The A|B|C methodology is an acronym for the words AUDIENCE - BRIDGES + BARRIERS - CHANGE.

It seeks to answer these 4 questions:
What do I want? **CHANGE**
Who am I talking to? **AUDIENCE**
Why might they say no? **BARRIERS**
How can I get them to say yes? **BRIDGES**

So if you follow the metaphor, the idea is to design **BRIDGES** to carry your **AUDIENCE** over the **BARRIERS** across to **CHANGE**. That's an oversimplification, of course, but it serves as a good background to the methodology.

Each of these steps will help you zero in on the key factors to consider and then will help suggest the right approach to optimize your chances of getting the result you want.

I'll give you a brief overview now of each aspect and then go through each step in detail in the following sections. There I'll give context, explanations, the scientific and psychological foundation for my assertions, and practical examples of how it has already worked with many of my clients. I'll also add some suggestions on how to apply the same principles in your next presentation to optimize the likelihood of success.

Before you would decide to cross a bridge, you would first choose your destination. So we will start with the final goal in mind. Instead of starting at A, we first consider C.

C stands for **CHANGE**. Every presentation should end in change. The accurate measure of a presentation's effectiveness is its success at changing your audience.

You need to be clear and focused on your end goal. I'll help you crystalize that later, but for now, you can think of it very simply. What Change(s) are you looking for after your presentation is over?

In the section on **CHANGE**, I go into two aspects to consider: PURPOSE AND PERCEPTION.

PURPOSE: What do you want your audience to think, feel, or do when your presentation is over? Such as approve, align, agree, etc.

PERCEPTION: How should your audience think of you? Such as professional, knowledgeable, trustworthy.

This changes with each audience and varies from company to company, country to country, culture to culture, and so on.

You can now start to think about both of these aspects of **CHANGE**. Don't worry, I'll give you clear support and guidance when you get to that section in the next chapter.

Once this is firmly established you can move on to the next step.

**A** stands for **AUDIENCE**. Here is where you do what I call an Audience Analysis Due Diligence Deep Dive. We are looking to get a 360-degree view of our audience. We want to get to know them as deeply as possible –even if we haven't met them face to face. I usually look at two levels: demographics and psychographics.

DEMOGRAPHICS: *What* is this person? Man or woman? Old or young? Rich or poor? Etc. This is just a preliminary step to get a surface view. Next, we go deeper...

PSYCHOGRAPHICS: *Who* is this person? What makes them tick? (What do they love?) What ticks them off? (What do they hate?)

What keeps them up at night? (Fears, doubts, and worries) What gets them out of bed in the morning? (Passion, purpose, and drive)

Knowing and understanding these things will help you tailor your message to your audience and choose the best persuasive strategy.

The next step will be where we start to develop a strategy. B stands for two things, **BARRIERS + BRIDGES.**

**BARRIERS** represent anything that would prevent or dissuade your audience from making the CHANGE you seek. Most presenters open their laptops and start to brainstorm all the reasons their audience should say yes. But the audience often knows these already or may not care. Why they might say no is often more critical. It's important to know this because if they have a preconceived judgment or decision in their head, consciously or subconsciously, it won't matter what we say until we address those specific concerns, reasons, or feelings.

I usually think of 4 different types of **BARRIERS**: Personal, Professional, Physical, and Psychological. (Full detailed explanation and analysis will be in the **BARRIERS** section.)

There is another B, and this is where we develop our strategy. The second B stands for **BRIDGES.**

**BRIDGES** are the well-thought-out structures, techniques, and angles you use to get your audience over their barriers. These include the principles of persuasion, behavioral science principles, strategic storytelling, humor, and many other psychological techniques we will cover in this book.

In sequence, the goal is to clearly figure out the **CHANGE** you want first, then analyze your target **AUDIENCE**, try to figure out what **BARRIERS** they have that prevent them from **CHANGE**, then figure out a strategy by designing and building **BRIDGES**, which represent your presentation, your communication intervention.

In the following chapters, I will go through these one by one in detail with many examples and suggestions on practically implementing the principles we will discuss.

This book can be considered as a kind of Choose Your Own Adventure book. By that I mean, if you just want to get to the psychology part, skip ahead to the **BRIDGES** section. It has all the applied persuasive psychology you want. After that you can circle back around and read the other parts in sequential order to get some more depth on the methodology.

If you want to explore the methodology in the correct sequence and detail, just proceed to the following section and I'll walk you methodically through the steps. I've designed this book to be part instructional, part reference, and part recreational (to keep the flow). Ultimately, I wrote this to be read in chronological order but I know that everyone has different styles and preferences. So read as you feel comfortable. I also made some sections as reference guides that you can come back to and use as a checklist of sorts to guide you through your next presentation. You can skim over it in the first reading and come back later to dive in deeper.

There will be points where I realize that some of you might be hesitating and are not buying into my methodology. At that point I'll have to openly address your doubts and explain the reasoning and basis for my assertions. If you are already a believer, you can skip those parts. But, honestly you might want to stick around because I've got some good examples to prove my points that might be of interest to you.

Takeaways

- The A|B|C persuasive presentation methodology is practical, principled, and psychological.

- Behavioral Science + Behavioral Economics are the study of judgment and decision-making.

- Decisions are made with both logic and emotions, but emotions are often the driving force.

- Presentations are the bridges that bring our audience to change.

# CHANGES: No sleep 'til Brooklyn

"A wise man bridges the gap by laying out the path by means of which he can get from where he is,to where he wants to go."

**J.P. Morgan**

T HE BRIDGE HAD JUST taken the life of Emily's father-in-law, John Roebling. He was the chief engineer and designer of the Brooklyn Bridge. A stoic, stern, and shrewd businessman. He was competent, capable, and confident. He pioneered modern bridge making and was famous at the time for his many marvelous engineering feats. He was commonly referred to as the "lesser Leonardo" (referring to Leonardo da Vinci).

He died an agonizing death – slow and painful. In a freak accident, his leg was crushed between the dock and an incoming ferry. Gangrene set in, and amputation was necessary. He suffered from complications from lockjaw (tetanus). After a month of pain and agony, he finally passed away. It was a very long month.

Emily's husband, Washington, John Roebling's son, had taken his place as chief engineer. Yet the Bridge was looking to claim its next victim. Washington Roebling now lay bedridden, paralyzed, and incapacitated. A mysterious illness had killed and maimed several laborers, and now this ailment had him fighting for his very life.

The mix of symptoms was unlike anything else experienced at the time. There were strange, unexplained mood changes, confusion, memory loss, incontinence, the sensation of tiny insects crawling over the skin, paralysis, bouts of unconsciousness, and often death.

For lack of a medical definition, they termed it Caissons Disease. A caisson was a large, waterproof wooden structure wherein laborers would work deep beneath the water. They would dig by hand through the sand to find bedrock to set the foundations of the Bridge.

The disease would go on to maim or kill over 20 more before the end of the project. But what was the cause of this bizarre illness? Some thought it was a poisonous substance they were coming into daily contact with down in those depths. Others felt it might be a toxic gas released from digging so deep below the surface. There were many guesses, but the real reason wouldn't be known until years after his death.

The Bridge was fraught with dangers and hidden hazards. Oversights and freak accidents were commonplace, and some felt the project was cursed. The Bridge claimed as many as 40 lives during its construction.

Emily Warren Roebling now had to not only care for her incapacitated husband, but also assume his duties as chief engineer of the greatest engineering feat of its time. She had to act as a liaison between him and the field engineers. She would collect his thoughts through dictation and then deliver them to the construction site. For all intents and purposes, she was the de facto chief engineer.

As Washington's condition worsened, he could only observe from his sickbed, propped up to look through a telescope aimed at the Bridge. He could barely move. He communicated with Emily through a rudimentary Morse code. Washington slowly and softly tapped out words, sentences, and even math equations on her arm. It was an excruciatingly slow and painful process.

She was a good student. She quickly learned about all the intricacies of the Bridge. She learned about the many machines and devices used in construction, and the workers that ran them. She studied complex mathematical formulas to understand the unique engineering concepts involved in the Bridge's design. She became an expert on all the unique materials used to build this colossal structure.

She also had to deal with the supervisors, the laborers, the vendors, the stakeholders, as well as the politicians. Each one came with its own set of unique challenges. She set out to learn their jobs, even as well as they did, so that she could field every question and solve every problem that arose.

An exceptionally bold and capable person, she was definitely up to the task. Yet not everyone agreed. The city council, led by the mayor himself, was planning to replace Washington Roebling as chief engineer due to his incapacitating ailments. The Bridge was also way over budget and behind schedule. Replacement seemed inevitable.

A meeting was called, and Emily would have to stand before the council and defend her husband's position. This would be a make-or-break presentation. This speech could either spell the end of the Roebling legacy or indelibly scribe the Roebling name into the annals of history. The outcome would determine if her husband, Washington Roebling, would stay on or be replaced as head engineer. This one speech could change history.

**A speech to change history**

Emily was a capable wife and a hard worker. She was also extremely dedicated to her family legacy and the Bridge itself. The Roeblings had conquered every challenge that stood before them and were afraid of nothing. The Bridge was now the focal point of the Roebling legacy.

She wasn't about to give up without a fight. She was known to be a master communicator – charming and diplomatic. She represented her husband, and thus the Roebling legacy, in a speech before the American Society of Civil Engineers.

At a time when women weren't allowed to wear pants, didn't have the right to vote, and didn't hold titles like "engineer," she needed to tread carefully when facing this male-dominated council.

There are no transcripts of this speech, but historians have painted the scene for us. As the story goes, they came to the part where they questioned Washington Roebling's physical condition and whether he was qualified to continue as head engineer. Using her intellect in conjunction with her charm, Emily made the case for her husband in a passionate and moving, yet logical and rational speech to the council and all onlookers.

The exact details of what was said in that speech are unknown. Historians say that her speech persuasively swayed the engineers in the room due to her confidence, conviction, and commitment. A vote was made, and the council voted in favor of keeping Washington as head engineer!

This was a significant success for the Roebling legacy, for women everywhere, and for the future of Emily and her beloved Bridge!

In the end, her preparation, passion, and persuasiveness won out. Metaphorically speaking, Emily's speech had spanned the gap between Brooklyn and Manhattan that day. Between an uncertain future for the Bridge project to a permanent place in history for Emily Roebling, and thus, the Roebling legacy.

Washington Roebling was still the head engineer, but in reality, this meant that Emily Warren Roebling would continue carrying out the lion's share of her husband's responsibilities. This would ultimately lead to her becoming, as is widely accepted, the first female engineer in history!

It is intriguing indeed that the fate of their legacy, the course of equal rights, and the outcome of the Bridge itself were teetering precariously on the outcome of that one speech, her history changing presentation. This one presentation was crucial for her future and her beloved Bridge.

C H-CH-CH-CH-CHANGES

Presentations are still as crucial as ever today. Your first job interview. Asking for a raise or a promotion. A progress update. A request for a follow-up meeting. Pitching your new startup to angel investors. Negotiating with your competition. A sales proposal. All these are forms of presentations in one way or another.

What can strategically designing and delivering persuasive presentations mean for you? How might optimizing your persuasiveness in presentations help your career, your projects, your reputation, and your relationships?

Although many people have given hundreds or even thousands of presentations, most don't have a clear strategy and have fallen into routine, automatic, and mechanical habits when it comes to presentation design and delivery.

You want to be confident, compelling, and convincing.
You want to see real changes after your presentation.
You want to persuade.

But you're not sure which content to include or highlight – or which to cut out. You're not sure how to design and deliver your message for maximum impact. You're worried that this will be just another waste of time and effort. You're afraid that this will be yet another boring data dump.

Every presentation should end with change. There's much truth to that, and I take that statement very literally. Every presentation should leave the audience in a different state than it found them.

So there's a need to take a different approach. There's a need to have a clear and simple methodology. A need for persuasive strategy. A need for change.

Imagine having real confidence in your presentation because you actually knew what you were doing when you designed it. Imagine how that confidence would feel. Imagine being able to control your nerves. Having a solid strategy and the principles to apply it will help you get over the fear of the unknown and the dreaded imposter syndrome. Imagine fear turning into excitement and anticipation as you look forward to your presentations. Imagine the confidence boost you will get when seeing real impact and results after your presentations.

Why do I say that? It's because we need to see presentations as unique opportunities.

What do you want to happen once the presentation is done? What do you want your audience to think, feel, or do?

It may sound like a simple question, but it's one of the questions that many of my clients don't initially think deeply enough about. Usually, there is a quick answer to that question that superficially and partially answers it, but we almost always need to go deeper.

Advertising mogul David Ogilvy is credited with saying, "People don't think how they feel, don't say what they think, and don't do what they say."

# Every presentation Should end with
# **change**

We often have trouble deciding on and articulating what we want. Our audiences are also sometimes not sure what they want, and that's OK. You can help them. But as a presenter, even if you don't have your life goals mapped out well, it's imperative that you clearly know what you want from each and every presentation.

"A presentation that doesn't seek to make change is a waste of time and energy." – Seth Godin

**CHANGE**? What **CHANGE** could you hope to achieve at the end of your presentation? Your answer might be simple at first. But as you'll see, like many of these questions we discussed, we need to go a bit deeper to have a clear and specific goal. Your first answer might be to sell, persuade, get approval, or inform. These are not bad in themselves but let's go deeper.

For example, my clients often say, "I just want to inform them of XYZ." Well, that's OK, but what is the **CHANGE** you want in them? I often counter this statement with the question, "What's the difference between your presentation and an email?" It's sobering but true.

If all we want is to simply convey data, an email is sufficient, and saves time and money. If you're just passing on information, that can be done without a presenter.

Just informing is not the ultimate goal for a presentation. You could have sent an email, memo, or printed out a handout instead of holding a meeting, and saved everybody time.

I have clients who have to fly halfway around the world just for one business presentation. Just imagine the cost of time spent traveling, car service to and from the airport, first-class flights, 5-star hotels and meals, etc. They aren't flown there to simply convey information. So why do they have to go through all of that and spend all these resources just for one presentation?

Presentations are about showing your competence, character, and confidence. Does your audience really trust you?

The board wants to see that you know your stuff, are sure you can pull it off, and believe in your heart what you are saying. They need to know that they can really trust you with their people, resources, and money.

Many of these in person visits have transitioned to online pre-sentations due to the Covid-19 pandemic. But rest assured that, whether virtual or in person, they are still looking for these same key indicators.

"People
don't
**think how they feel,**
don't
**say what they think,**
and don't
**do what they say."**

- David Ogilvy

So let's think of what emotional factors may be involved. For example, I worked with one company, and the director said he was frustrated that no one was following a protocol on the newly implemented software. The director said he had sent emails with clear instructions; they had a presentation on introducing the software and live demos to show how to do it; he had met with many and walked them through the process. Yet few had adopted the new software and switched over. He was frustrated because he couldn't understand why his team was so incompetent.

Digging further, I quickly realized that everyone knew what to do and had no problem grasping the basic concepts of the new software. The problem was that no one *wanted* to do it. There were many possible reasons for this. It could be an attitude problem, a bad past experience, a laziness or comfort zone factor, etc. So until that emotional issue was addressed, the mechanics of that problem were inconsequential.

Trust is based on emotions as well as logic. So as a presenter, it's good to leverage the emotional advantage of presentations.

Likewise, if you're trying to teach something, then your goal might be to impart knowledge and have them remember what you said. But if you actually want people to do what you taught them, you might have to inspire or motivate them. This would involve changing their attitude and present state of mind. Yes, sometimes we need to dig a little deeper because more than just conveying information is involved.

So one thing you have to realize is that it's important to think of any potential **BARRIERS** that might prevent them from implementing, agreeing with, understanding, being physically able to, or wanting to use your information. So mere transfer of information should not be the entire goal of a presentation.

**Purpose and Perception**

So we will look at two aspects of **CHANGE** you need to consider before designing your next communication intervention: Purpose and Perception.

## PURPOSE

What is the underlying purpose of your presentation? What do you want your audience to think, feel, or do? In the example we just saw, the engineers weren't switching over to the new software. It wasn't as simple as just understanding how to switch over. That wasn't the problem.

It's the same with sales. Every salesperson knows the customer isn't just buying the product or service. Listing off all the benefits is not what top salespeople do. No, they sell an idea, a value, an ideology, an identity, and often they must sell themselves first. The customer or client needs to trust them – or at the very least like them.

So let's say that you're trying to sell something in your presentation. The common thing to do would be to tell them everything they could gain by purchasing your product. It's likely they already know about these things or maybe aren't interested. Your true goal is in finding out what they ultimately want and then aligning your product or service with that vision. This takes questions, discernment, and insights.

But first, they may need to trust us. So a possible **CHANGE** for our presentation is building trust and rapport. Now, this is much harder than just listing off benefits and features. Anyone can do that.

Getting someone to feel and believe that you are trustworthy and reliable is a difficult goal for a presentation. Trust takes a long time to build up, right? Yet that is exactly what we need to do.

So how do we get people to trust us through a presentation? It's not an easy task, for sure, but it's possible. We will get to that when we get to **BRIDGES**.

What are some possible changes that we could target? I usually think of them as verbs or verb phrases, something that would happen after or even during the presentation. So start with a verb and end with some specific phrase that you would like to see.

What do you want your audience to Think, Feel, or Do?

For example, change their mind, change their attitude, change their behavior. You might want to...
Inspire your team, motivate employees, or hit a deadline.
Convince your audience that something is true, possible, and worthwhile.
Instill knowledge in a way that is memorable and inspiring.

So please pause here and take a moment and think about your last presentation, an upcoming presentation, or even a hypothetical future one. Think about what you want to accomplish. What is the change that you were seeking? Write down three words that describe the change you want.

You can use the examples below or any other ones you feel fit. So as an exercise now, please put down the book and come up with three sentences starting with "I want my audience to (insert change here)."

Now the temptation is to come up with what WE want to tell them. One of the common things I see with my clients is this need to tell the audience everything they know or about topics they know a lot about. But the real challenge is first to identify exactly what you want them to do, and then you will know what information they will need to hear to make that decision successfully.

For example, "I want to tell them about the new product." That's OK, just dig a little deeper to get to the effect you want on them. For example, you could say, "I want them to be excited about our product." Forming the purpose statement this way raises the obvious next question: How can I get them excited about my product? Now you're in a state of mind to problem-solve. Now you can line up what your audience naturally gets excited about with your message. Now you can look at your content, vocabulary, and delivery and decide if it elicits the kind of excitement you need.

Here are a few other examples of changes we might seek to spark your thinking. The complete list would be a book of its own. I usually like to think of this as a verb, an action.

Change their mind
Understand my concept
Agree with my ideas
Buy into my proposal
Approve the budget

Now that you have some purpose sentences, your design considerations should all support your purpose goals. Every word you say, every gesture you make, every inflection of your voice, every illustration, every slide; everything will be focused on making that change.

As you go through your presentation, you can keep referring back to these words and ask yourself if you've gone off track, started speaking about irrelevant things, or missed your points altogether. Or worse, you might find that you're doing the opposite of what you want, inadvertently making it harder for them to make that change.

It's good to remember that often there are multiple things that we might want. We might want to sell something, but we will also want our audience feeling good about the purchase. That way, they will return for more in the future, write a good review, tell their friends and colleagues about us, and become loyal clients or customers. So you might add points or information that starts to build a relationship.

Also, we should realize that we often can't get all we want in one presentation or pitch. Sometimes we have to plan a strategic buildup to what we ultimately want.

For example, we might want to sell someone an expensive piece of equipment or a pricey service. When these are very expensive, we can rarely sell them after a brief conversation or after showing a PowerPoint presentation. On our first go, we might have the goal of building rapport, building trust. Once we have built trust, we might go on to invite them for a tour of the factory or a live demo. Then in a future presentation we might pitch the sale. Later we will go on to possibly negotiate the sale. So we might have to plan out different phases for reaching our goals.

Take a few minutes to scan this list and write down some **CHANGES** you might want in future presentations. Feel free of course to add your own!

REFERENCE PURPOSE LIST

# A
Accept: an idea, a value, an offer
Accomplish: a task, a project
Achieve: a goal, a dream, an ideal
Acknowledge: a fault, a weakness, a mistake
Acquire: knowledge, wisdom, and power
Agree: on an offer, a compromise, a direction, a plan
Align: on a decision, direction, or process
Apply: information, methodology, process, philosophy
Appreciate: a person, a role, a team, a rule, a legacy, a tradition, a culture
Approve: a plan, a project, a budget, a decision, a change
Assure: quality, timing, process, legalities
Authorize: spending, role, decision
Avoid: actions, thinking, feeling, attitude, dangers, risk


# B

**Believe**: a fact, a person, data, a narrative
**Build**: respect, rapport, relationship, trust
**Buy/sell**: a product or service


# C

**Care**: for policy, morals, ethics, principles, guidelines
**Change**: mind, attitude, actions
**Choose**: an idea, a service, a product, a process, an option

**Commit**: to a role, habit, action
**Communicate**: concerns, feelings, thoughts, feedback
**Consider**: an alternative, an option, counterpoints
**Contribute**: donations, ideas, feedback
**Cooperate**: with a team, partner, client, company culture
**Correct**: habit, action, mistake
**Cut**: costs, spending, losses, waste

# D

**Decide**: options, choices, purchases
**Demonstrate**: value, reliability, benefits, consequences
**Determine**: direction, methodology, an issue
**Discover**: opportunities, root problems, causes
**Discuss**: underlying issues, trouble areas

# E

**Eliminate**: conflict, misunderstandings
**Encourage**: conduct, habits, traits
**Expand**: dialogue, understanding,
**Experience**: a feeling, a sensation, a situation, reality
**Express**: regret, appreciation, sorrow, pride, shame

# F

**Fix**: a behavior, an issue, a mistake
**Follow**: rules, guidelines, leadership

# G-H

**Gain**: ability, knowledge, confidence, hope
**Generate**: ideas, excitement, anticipation
**Grow**: insights, experience

# I

**Imagine:** possibilities, potential, success
**Implement:** initiatives, processes, procedures
**Impress:** superiors, clients, colleagues
**Improve:** team spirit, morale, process
**Increase:** output, morale, efficiency, effectiveness

# J-L

**Join:** a team, a club, an organization, a company
**Learn:** a skill, a process, a philosophy

# M-O

**Maintain:** conduct, spirit, perception
**Meet:** deadlines, requirements

# P-Q

**Participate:** in a conversation, activities, a discussion, a project
**Promote:** culture, spirit, behavior
**Propose:** a plan, a direction

# R

**Raise:** funds, capital, their hands, their fists
**Reach:** agreement, consensus, a goal, a decision
**Realize:** the truth, an issue, fault, an opportunity, value
**Recall:** the past, a mistake, success, a feeling
**Reduce:** costs, spending, loss, bad habits
**Reflect:** on the past, concepts, ideals, values, morals
**Regret:** mistakes, lost opportunity, decisions
**Relate:** to a feeling, a situation, or a state of being
**Remember:** a fact, a principle, methodology

**Renew**: a commitment, a promise, a vow, identity
**Replace**: goals, values, morals
**Resolve**: internal debates, arguments, contradictions
**Review**: current situation, past successes and failures

## S

**Share**: ideas, stories, case studies, knowledge
**Show**: proof of concept, viability
**Solve**: an issue, an argument, a problem
**Start/stop**: an action, a process, a habit, a lead item, a behavior, an attitude, a dialogue
**Support**: a decision, the team, a role, a partner

## T-Z

**Teach**: a concept, a belief, a methodology
**Think**: differently about an issue
**Trust**: a person (including you), a team, a product, a service, a company, an organization, a methodology
**Try**: something new, an alternative
**Understand**: a concept, a methodology, a decision, a direction, a narrative
**Update**: a project, requirements, a scope
**Value**: company culture, opposing viewpoints

# What's the difference between your Presentation and an Email?

So that is what we call our purpose. It's what we want the other person to think, feel, or do.

Now we will get into the next point, which is commonly overlooked in most presentation design preparation. We want to think about what perception the audience has about us when we are finished.

## PERCEPTION

There are certain things about how we are perceived that we can't change. For example, our race, age, height, years of experience. Unfortunately, people could have a bias either for us or against us because of some of these factors. But there are many things that we can deliberately control to affect their view of us.

So think for a moment about what things you would like to change regarding perception. This will change from audience to audience, just like our purpose will. How we would like to be perceived by our superior will differ from our colleagues, subordinates, or clients. We can also look at this part as a sort of personal branding. What is it that you want to be known for? When you are done speaking, how would you like to be described?

Now let's take that a step further. Let's not just think about how we want to be seen but how our audience needs to see us.

The way we talk to a romantic interest is different from how we talk to our children, to someone else's children, to our parents, to our siblings, to our close friends, to our subordinates, to our colleagues, to our superiors.

There are many aspects to our personality and many sides to our communication styles. Yes, we use different tones, vocabulary, body language, expressions, sense of humor, and stories with different types of people in everyday life. Yet often I see people use only one presentation voice/personality. If we want people to be receptive to our message, it's important that we speak in a way they like and respect. This is not being fake or inauthentic. Instead, this is a way of showing respect to those we are talking to by adapting to their preferred style.

Each audience might need to see a different side of us, or for us to show that side more prominently, to make the change we desire. It's also important that our communication style doesn't detract from our message, rather than attract people to it.

I usually like to think of these words as adjectives or nouns. So think for a minute about your last presentation, an upcoming one, or even a hypothetical one. Think about your audience and how you would like to be perceived by them – and then how they would like or need to perceive you. Sometimes these two things are the same, and sometimes they are vastly different. If we would like to be seen as spontaneous, creative, and witty, yet our boss appreciates someone serious, conscientious, and structured – there is a potential issue.

Now think of your audience and the way they need to perceive you to partake in the kind of **CHANGE** you want them to make. There may be some differences, and there may be some areas where our wants and their needs clash.

We can look back at the cues from the first section of this book. How might we need to be perceived by...
A leader? Resourceful, innovative, and diligent. A problem-solver.
A client? Honest, trustworthy, and knowledgeable. A partner.
A colleague? Cooperative, collaborative, and down to earth. A team player.
A subordinate? Approachable, supportive, and helpful. A mentor.

A word of caution, it's easy to get this wrong on the first take, so as you go along in the next days, weeks, months, and even years, you might change these words drastically.

For example, one time I was helping a client prepare for a big speech in front of her new company to introduce herself. She was replacing the former HR head of the APAC region. So as we went through the A|B|C process I asked her how she would like to be perceived. She thought for a moment and said, "I want to be perceived as a bold, powerful, and strong woman. A leader who is in control. I want them to know that I'm knowledgeable and competent and have the strength to be a leader in their company."

I had known this woman for some time and worked with her for years so I knew her personality very well. It didn't seem like these were the first words I would use to describe her, even though she truly possessed all these qualities and abilities. It just didn't seem like that really described her true core. So I asked her more questions to find out and dig deeper into what she was trying to do.

I asked about the woman that she was replacing. It turns out that everyone in the company disliked the woman. She left because she was a bad fit and didn't align with the company culture. On further questioning, she admitted the executive was, in effect, driven out of the company.

When I asked about this former executive and what she was like she replied, "Umm, they said she was bold, powerful, and strong."

"Hmm, sounds like the words you just chose. So are these the qualities you really want to put front and center – even though you possess them?" I asked.

"No!" she quickly replied, "I guess not." After a few moments of thought, she said, "I want them to know that I am caring and nurturing. I believe in work-life balance and put my family first and foremost above everything. Also, I view the people I work with as my extended family, so I want them to feel that we all need to care for each other and that I'll be there for them when they need me. I want them to feel that I'm approachable and that if they see me in the hallways, they should not hesitate to say hi, come up to me, ask me a question, visit my office, or say what's really on their mind. That my door is always open!"

"Wow! Now that's more like it!" I said.

When we designed the speech, we made it lighthearted and humorous and sprinkled it with compassion and kindness. There were even a few self-deprecating jokes to show her new team that she was approachable and didn't take herself too seriously.

At the same time, we highlighted her strengths, so the audience realized her competence and abilities without directly listing them off like a menu.

We put in a few stories that subtly let them know that she was capable and had very successful relationships with people at many different levels. We also showed that she could be strong, independent, bold, and brave when needed.

I spoke to her afterward, and she said that it went extremely well. The feedback was better than she had imagined, and she was thrilled that she didn't go with her first reaction to my question. Her audience got a good idea of her true personality.

Afterwards, many later came up to her in the hallway to introduce themselves, saying that normally they don't do things like that. But, she came across as so friendly, so approachable, that they felt comfortable with her and could just be themselves around her. But that feeling wasn't accidental. The content and delivery was carefully designed and engineered to let her best traits shine through.

Exercise: So take a moment and come up with 3 to 6 words you would like to define yourself when you're done with this presentation. And just like with your purpose, once you have chosen these words, you can look at your presentation and ask yourself if its current iteration aligns with those words.

For example, if you say "confident." Are you using decisive words or more tentative words like "maybe," "seems like," "perhaps"? Are you using a lot of filler words like "umm," "ugh," "ah," that betray your confidence? Does your body language betray your inner confidence? Does your voice belie the image that you're calm, cool, and confident?

If you chose the word "professional," does your presentation look professional? Does your appearance look professional according to what your audience deems professional? Does your slide deck look professional? Is it cutesy because you filled in all the white-space with a picture of pink kittens, or does it resemble the McKinsey-type slides that your superior holds as the gold standard?

If you said "logical," you can ask, "Did I explain this in an orderly, structured way that would make someone think that I'm logical? Is there a clear sequence that screams logical, structured, and organized??"

If you said, "a team player," do you sound like you are sharing the credit for everything? Have you highlighted team accomplishments and phrased things with "we" instead of "I"? Does the way you present the information sound like you're focusing everything on your successes and strengths, or does it come across as a team effort, thus falling in line with "team player"?

Don't rush this step and don't be afraid to modify these from time to time as you find they have changed, don't reflect what you want accurately, or are not serving your needs any longer. Once these changes are chosen and clarified, we can move on to the next step.

Takeaways

- Every presentation should end with change.

- PURPOSE: What do you want your audience to think, feel, or do?

- PERCEPTION: How do you want your audience to perceive you? Then balance that with... How does your audience need to perceive you in order to change?

# AUDIENCES: DEMOS & PSYCHOS

## "The wisdom of bridges comes from the fact that they know both sides...!"

### Mehmet Murat ildan

Let's go back to Emily's speech before the council. Imagine Emily standing before this daunting group of prestigious men. She was an extremely bold and confident woman. As she put it, years later, in an 1898 letter to her son: "I have more brains, common sense, and know-how generally than have any two engineers, civil or uncivil, and but for me, the Brooklyn Bridge would never have had the name Roebling in any way connected with it!" She was definitely not lacking in the confidence department.

She was also brilliant. She graduated with top honors from the Georgetown Visitation convent academy in Washington, D.C. , where she excelled in science and algebra. She also carried so much responsibility and decision-making on the construction site that people were starting to wonder if she was the real brains behind the bridge.

Washington Roebling fell in love with Emily at first sight. He wrote of her in a letter to his sister in 1865: "Some people's beauty lies not in the features, but in the varied expression that the countenance will assume under the various emotions. She is... a most entertaining talker, which is a mighty good thing, you know, I myself being so stupid."

OK, admittedly not romantic by today's standards, but you can easily see that he fell in love with both body and mind when he met her. He was taken by both her intellect and her charm. Yes, she was a great speaker. She was known to be charming, eloquent, and articulate.

But could she convince the council that things should continue as they were? There were rumors Washington was losing his mind. People hadn't seen him in public for some time, and some wondered if he was even still alive. Emily had to consider her situation carefully. She had to consider her audience's perception of her.

There were cultural considerations to consider. At that time, it wasn't considered normal for a woman to speak in public as it is now in most cultures. Would her bold natural style be met with applause or condemnation? Again, we don't know what was said in that room that day.

But naturally, we can assume that she didn't try to tell them that she had twice as much brains, know-how, and common sense as anyone in the room!

Yes, she was smart, she was able to put her ego aside and found a message, a tone, and a delivery that achieved her goals. She considered her audience and it paid off.

O BSERVANCE, RECONNAISSANCE, AND DUE **diligence**

Everyone has heard that the audience is king or queen, #1, the sole reason for the presentation, etc. But what does that really mean when designing and delivering a presentation?

The typical starting point is doing a basic demographic breakdown. Demographics, while helpful, are merely a starting point for our audience analysis. Doing research, real research will help to find out more.

Demographics usually tend to focus on WHAT the person is. By that I mean, a title, a category, and often this may include a stereotype. For example, man or woman? Young or old? Rich or poor? Educated or uneducated? Married or single? Local or foreigner? Expert or newbie?

There is a great meme on the internet of Prince (now King) Charles and Ozzy Osbourne. If you look at some of their demographics, they are extremely similar. They are both the same age, from the same area, rich, famous, live in a castle, married twice etc. Yet obviously, these somewhat similarities don't mean that these two are similar in tastes, personality, styles, opinions, etc.

Preliminary demographics are fine if that's all you have access to. But we can take a step further to establish who they are. This is where we get into psychographics. Think of psychographics as an Audience Analysis Due Diligence Deep Dive!

Psychographics are concerned with WHO this person is at the core. What keeps them up at night? What gets them out of bed in the morning? What makes them tick? What ticks them off? We need to find out as much as possible within reason, within the scope of the law, and of course with ethics in mind.

Psychographics came into public awareness in 2016 when the Facebook/Cambridge Analytica scandal occurred. Cambridge Analytica was caught using data from a Facebook online personality test. This broke Facebook's terms of service and led to a public inquiry. This is a great example of unethical use of personal information.

# Think of psychographics as an
# Audience analysis
# Due diligence
# Deep dive

They used a basic personality test known as the Big 5, or OCEAN. This test determines the scale of 5 different aspects of your personality. We can briefly look at this test as it's a good starting point to finding out more about our audience. OCEAN is an acronym — Openness, Conscientiousness, Extraversion, Agreeableness, and Neuroticism.

There are plenty of online tests you can use to determine your own values. Once you get the hang of the type of questions and answers that point to a higher or lower score in one trait, you can start to guess what other people's scores might be. This is only a guess, of course, but it will bring you closer to understanding who they are and what drives them.

What do they like, or dislike? What have they done, or not done? We can look at blogs, emails, speeches, videos, newsletters, interviews, etc. When we study these things, we can look for patterns in speech, expressions they commonly use, personal concepts and philosophies, deeply held beliefs, and also personal interests and hobbies. Later when we are creating our presentation, we can sprinkle in references to these things in our words, expressions, and stories.

Now, if you feel this may come across as creepy or stalker-like, let me put your mind at ease.

Think of it like going on a job interview. There is nothing an interviewer wants to see less than potential job candidates walking in with no knowledge of the company or its culture. On the contrary, the more they know and express about the company, and particularly how they will fit in and be a real benefit to the company, the better. How can they say they're a good fit and will really be an asset if they don't know anything about the company, its goals, or its culture? If they don't really understand what the company does, where it came from, and where it wants to go, how can they say that they will be of benefit?

The more personalized it is, the better. The more generic it is, well, I think you get the point.

It's the same with your audience. How can you promise that your content is in their best interests if you don't know exactly what those interests are? How can you say that your product will satisfy them when you don't know their personal criteria for satisfaction?

OK, sometimes I get pushback on this part so if you're still on the fence here, please consider the following examples. The purpose of these examples is to show you that people in general are actually very impressed and often touched when you do your homework and put some effort to find out more about them than mere surface demographics.

## Lessons from the human serviette

There is a notorious music industry reporter named John Ruskin. He is better known as Nardwuar. He has interviewed such celebrities as Nirvana, Sonic Youth, Lady Gaga, Katy Perry, Jay-Z, and even the likes of Mikhail Gorbachev.

He casts quite an eccentric figure. He dresses in bizarre, mismatched clothing, seemingly sourced from the Salvation Army thrift shop. He often dons an oversized beret, in a bold tartan pattern, with a big pom on top. He speaks in an irritating, nasally whining voice. In interviews, he usually asks silly or straight-out strange questions. He calls himself "the human serviette" (napkin in American English).

A writer from *The New York Times* described him this way: "My favorite journalist is a shrieking British Columbian who dresses like an exploded 1970s Soviet golf catalog... I couldn't believe what he was showing me: an obnoxious young man accosting musicians I held in high regard, who was only rarely physically assaulted for his impertinence. I thought it was all an act, the sort of high-wire disingenuousness that would later be perfected by Sacha Baron Cohen."—from Nardwuar's website.

As you can imagine, this type of interview style might not sit well with most busy musicians and celebrities who don't have a lot of time, have already gone through multiple interviews that day, and have seen and heard it all. And yes, this has gotten him into more than a few altercations, with some musicians at the point of physically threatening him or even taking a swing at him. I admit, I also find his style of communication quite irritating.

So why is this odd character still around and so well known (and often admired and loved) by the music industry? What is his saving grace?

One thing Nardwuar prides himself in is his detailed and thorough research. He will dig deep to unearth facts and details from the artist's past. He will often reference their early school memories, old flames, and early projects long forgotten. He will even try to find an old souvenir from their past as a gift.

In an interview with Snoop Dogg, Nardwuar presented him with the first VHS movie he made in 1996. Snoop was amazed and whistled with excitement and then said, "Oh my... This is ...what I've been trying to find!"

Singer Pharrell Williams was gifted with an ultra-rare vinyl copy of his first-ever recording. Pharrell was shocked! He paused for a few seconds and slowly said, "This is... this is... This is one of the most impressive interviews I've ever experienced in my life. Seriously... this is insane!" Later in the same interview, Pharrell said, "Your research is second to none. Second to none."

Another person who excels at this is Sean Evans. If you're unfamiliar with him, he is the host of a YouTube channel called Hot Ones.

The premise of the show is pure genius. It's basically a mix between an interview and a food tasting show.

He lines up a row of 10 chicken wings, each with a different hot sauce.

Each wing gets incrementally hotter. As he and the guest start to eat a wing, he will ask them a question. As you can imagine, as the wings get hotter, it gets harder and harder to answer, and the guests sometimes even struggle to speak. Simultaneously, his questions get hotter and hotter.

Evans has interviewed many celebrities, including Shaquille O'Neal, Ed Sheeran, Justin Timberlake, Billie Eilish, Matt Damon, Kevin Hart, Kristen Stewart, Gordon Ramsey, Post Malone, Neil deGrasse Tyson, Scarlett Johansson, Noel Gallagher, and Jimmy Kimmel.

But what really sets the show apart is Sean's thorough research and well-thought-out questions. He will reference something from their lives that they thought no one would ever know. The look on their faces, the shock and surprise, the instant respect for him, and the smiles say it all. And then comes the flood of compliments. "This was the best interview ever!" "You really do your homework!" "I'm so impressed with you right now!"

He recently did some interviews where he explained his methodology and process. "I think if it were just people reacting to spicy wings all the time, it would get old to people pretty quick... So  the research process, which is basically like, we read everything, we watch everything. We make sure that we watch the whole film catalog and read almost everything that's in print. We'll try to track down what their local papers were saying about them early on, before their careers were ever big, because those are probably people that would know them best. We try to go to the roots of everything. And now you have so much podcast material and all these interviews on YouTube, you have these back catalogs on the internet...

"We then create a research dossier out of all the interesting nuggets that we find. Then we kind of combine these dossiers together and we'll come up with maybe like 30 talking points that we could hit. We'll narrow that down to what we think are the most interesting 10, and then those will each be different wings... So, yeah. I've never really thought about it, but yeah, it does give me a kind of unique perspective into these people's worlds and lives..."

"Growing up, I had heroes in Howard Stern and Jimmy Kimmel, in David Letterman, Adam Corolla... I think nowadays, if I look in the internet space, Nardwuar was a huge inspiration. I remember watching his videos when I was in college and just running back these super human moments when he would connect with certain people. I'd play them over and over... I take it as a huge compliment when fans tell me that they do the same thing with me, because I remember what that feeling was like..."

So my point in sharing these examples is that you will find that people appreciate it and respect you when you do your homework.

I'm not talking about going through someone's garbage or doing a stakeout with binoculars in a van with black-tinted windows across the street from their house. If you do those things, you are creepy, a stalker, and most likely a criminal.

A quick internet search will often yield helpful details that will help you to understand your audience. This is public information and often information they put out in interviews, blogs, articles, etc. A quick phone call to someone else that works or deals with your audience can be a treasure trove of valuable insights. And often, they don't even have to know that you did your research.

For example, I once had a client who had to give a presentation for her CEO in America. She was located in Shanghai, China, and was unfamiliar with the CEO. She was very nervous and asked me what she should say, how she should say it, and what things would be important.

So I asked her what she knew about him, and she said nothing except some vague demographics. Among other questions, I asked her if there was anything written about him. She told me that he had written a book about himself – an autobiography. It so happened that he had gifted it to her when visiting once. But she had never opened it. So we cracked it open and dug into who he was and what he stood for. It turned out that this book was recognized as a business textbook for many colleges and universities. It was a goldmine!

We found that, among other things, in high school and college, he was a star player for his football team. Now that he was older, he no longer played but was still very passionate about football. He even donated several million dollars to the athletic department at his alma mater! The book had many references to his passion for football.

So we designed the presentation in a way that tastefully and subtly included a few football idioms. Expressions like "moving the ball down the field," "dropping the ball," "kick-off," etc. These words would resonate with him, have a familiar ring, and evoke very positive and exciting emotions. She was speaking his language.

Standard advertising and marketing will yield you standard demographics, and there are many presentation gurus that recommend making persona cards that represent either certain people or groups of people in your audience. Well, this is a good start, but I encourage people to go deeper and find out as much as possible about your specific audience, especially as your audience gets smaller and more important. After all, very few of us are giving TED Talks to inspire thousands of people at once. Usually, our big presentations are for a very small group. It'll be for our clients, superiors, or other C suite executives, stakeholders, and decision-makers.

A few years ago, I had a client who was the president of a very large Fortune 500 company. This company has a yearly revenue of over $25 billion USD and operates in over 150 countries! He needed to fly from Shanghai to New York City to give a presentation to his board of directors to outline the strategy for the upcoming year. This was at the very beginning stages of the Covid-19 pandemic so there was a lot of uncertainty and worry.

When I researched his board of directors, I was amazed! They were CEOs and ex-CEOs, and vice presidents of other equally huge companies. They collectively had centuries of experience and knowledge. I had never given a speech to a board of directors of that caliber. They were definitely out of my league. But with a bit of basic research we could pick out different qualities, philosophies, and personalities of each board member. We could also see which ones would most likely agree or disagree with certain ideas and concepts. So we could imagine and prepare for points they might bring up in disagreement. We were also able to target certain messages to them.

To great effect, we found areas where my client's strategy lined up with strategies that some of them had used in the past. We were able to create moments where he could point to them by name and say, "'XXX, remember in 2008 when you guided your company through the financial crisis? Well, I'm taking a move from your strategy playbook this year and applying it to our situation." Now realistically, XXX is not likely to poke holes in this since it's also his strategy. To the contrary, he will most likely defend it if others happen to criticize it. In this way, he could assure the board that everything was under control and his strategy was solid.

These days you can find out so much about someone online. They most often have willingly made it available. It's a great chance to know who you will be facing ahead of time.

**Getting professional about getting personal**

Here are a few different aspects you can consider. You can look at the different aspects of who they are.

PROFESSIONAL: Their position, experience, knowledge, successes, mistakes, past positions, emails and messages they've written, blogs, podcasts, YouTube videos, memos, books, magazine articles, interviews, etc. Videos are preferred because you can get a better feel for their personality, communication style, and disposition.

PERSONAL: Personality, opinions, background, marital status and family, religion, political leanings, likes and dislikes, hobbies, charities and causes or even protests and movements that they are affiliated with. Hobbies are always a good thing to know because once you know someone's passion, you can possibly find mutual interests. You can also look for ways to weave the topic into the presentation.

Recently I was waiting for a client to join a Zoom call and I decided to look her up on LinkedIn. I could see that all her posts, likes, and comments were focused on equal rights issues. Feminism was her main point of focus. In our call I was giving an example on how to tailor our message to our audience. In my illustration I said, "Imagine you're giving a presentation to the CEO and *she...*"

Because I knew her feelings on the topic, I could tailor my hypothetical story to her by choosing to make the CEO a woman instead of a man. This was an easy choice for me that would probably have gone unnoticed by her consciously yet might have been picked up subconsciously. Again, this would resonate with her and keep our interaction positive in her mind.

After the illustration I told her that I looked her up first and adapted my story specifically for her. She instantly realized the power of having knowledge of someone and using it discerningly. A little knowledge can have great power when used wisely.

People's personal passions, experiences, and feelings often affect them more deeply than their professional ones. Often these two seemingly separate parts of their lives converge in who they are and how they will react.

For example, a few years ago, in Shanghai, there was a meeting of two successful entrepreneurs, Jack Ma of Alibaba fame and Elon Musk of Tesla and SpaceX. These are considered to be two of the most successful and richest people in the world.

Suppose you had to give a presentation to Jack Ma of Alibaba. From the outside, you would see that he's one of the wealthiest men in the world and runs one of the most successful companies on the planet. So you might feel that you need to come in strong to show him that you are also competent and worthy of his attention and investment of time.

Yet, a quick bit of research would reveal that he had a history of rejection and always stresses the need for endurance and persever-ance. He was rejected many times for jobs and by organizations. He was rejected by his local police and by Harvard University; he failed his college entrance exam three times; he was overlooked for a job at a local hotel, and of course his favorite anecdote, when he went to KFC for a job with 26 other applicants, and only he got rejected!

Now knowing this, you might want to change your strategy. You might want to show him how you have faced rejection, made mistakes, suffered, yet gotten back up, learned from your past, and fell forward, as the expression goes. This would resonate with him to his core. Once you can find common ground on a deeper level, you've gotten that foot in the door, as it were.

How about Elon Musk? We know that he's a very ambitious guy that never surrenders and always has many irons in the fire when it comes to innovations, inventions, or industries. What do you know about him? What gets his attention?

Years ago in Shanghai, a singer came through and played a concert at a small, local venue. She was a really unique individual with a very funky style in clothing and appearance. It was a great show in an intimate setting with only a few hundred people. Her stage name was Grimes. If you were to tell me that this time next year, she'd be dating Elon Musk, I would never have believed you.

Yet, a little research reveals that Elon is also pretty eccentric. Apparently, he wanted to make a post on an obscure topic and searched to see if anyone else had posted on this before. It turns out Grimes beat him to it. He was impressed and wrote her. The rest is history. This one girl caught his attention because of his high interest in an obscure topic. Anyone who wanted to get the ear of Elon Musk could do it if they knew what he was passionate about. We need to delve deeper past the superficial. What if you knew your audience's deep passions and personal topics of interest?

Similarly, famous ex-FBI hostage negotiator turned author (Never split the difference) Chris Voss displays a tough exterior. No doubt he is tough. But he has said in interviews that he most likely became a cop  because he was often bullied when he was very young. This led to him having an increased awareness of injustice and oppression. He later joined a suicide hotline to help people, then became a hostage negotiator. In his masterclass he clearly states how much he hates bullies!

To really know what motivates people to do or not do things takes some unearthing. It takes research, and it takes questions. You never know what things someone will find interesting and react positively to. Outside of knowing someone personally, doing a little research might reveal some aspects that can be considered when you're later choosing your style of approach. As you learn more about your audience, think of ways they may resist the CHANGE you want.

Takeaways

- To understand more than just your audience's needs and wants, you need to do an Audience Analysis Due Diligence Deep Dive!

- Demographics tell <u>what</u> a person is (man or woman, old or young, etc.).

- Psychographics tell us <u>who</u> a person is (idealist, dreamer, spiritual, logical, etc. pain).

- Personal traits include hobbies, passions, likes/dislikes, fears and dreams, and pain points.

- Professional information includes business philosophy, experience, knowledge, successes and failures, and goals.

# BARRIERS:
## GEPHYROPHOBIA & METATHESIOPHOBIA

**"We build too many walls and not enough bridges."**

**Isaac Newton**

Manhattan was busy, bustling, and burgeoning in 1860. It was many things. It was the economic, industrial, and cultural center of America. And it was the third largest city in the whole world at the time. But it was not cheap to live in or easy to access.

Brooklyn, on the other hand, was inexpensive and easy to access. Around 40% of the working people in Brooklyn worked in Manhattan. They had to cross the East River every day for work. But how?

Before there was a bridge, you had to take a ferry across the Hudson River to get to Manhattan from Brooklyn. These ferries ran back and forth all day and late into the night. There were over 1,000 trips in a day. The trips were often rough, slow, and the traffic on the river was brutal. There were many accidents, mechanical failures, and inclement weather was common. It was far from pleasant or convenient.

There was often talk of building a bridge, but not many considered it a practical reality. Building a bridge there would be difficult, dangerous, and the price would be dear. It was a very long span across.

The idea for a bridge was loosely pitched and often talked about among city dwellers. But it was also controversial and hotly contested. There were a few issues to consider.

VIABILITY: Could this be physically achieved, or would this be a colossal waste of money?

SAFETY: Would this be just another catastrophe waiting to happen?

COST: Would this bankrupt the city or increase taxes?

These doubts and arguments swirled around like the river's eddies and currents below.

Safety was a key issue and people were scared. At that time, one out of four bridges were failing. The engineering and construction of long-span bridges were still in the very early stages. Miscalculations, inferior materials, and construction shortcuts took a heavy toll on the reputation and trust of these behemoth monoliths.

Public opinion was critical in the decision-making process. Staying aware of how the people felt was crucial in getting approval for and investment in a project as big as the Brooklyn Bridge. Those public officials approving it were taking a chance: they could be forever known as the hero behind an architectural landmark's success or the zero that said yes to the deaths of hundreds of people.

Yet, the people had dreams of a life easier lived. They wanted convenience, they wanted luxuries, they wanted the freedom to move around as they wished. The local government had dreams of positioning itself as the center of the free world. A bridge that would be the highest structure in North America would confirm any claims.

Gauging public opinion was not easy.

What exactly did the people dream of? What did they fear?
What facts did they need to hear?
Did they need the engineering calculations explained to them?
Did they need a physical demonstration?
Did they require an inspiring story to move and motivate them?
Was this the right time for change?

One day a providential event occurred that facilitated change.
On January 18, 1867, the weather changed suddenly, and the temperature dropped drastically. The whole river slowly froze over,
making it impossible to ferry across. Historically the river had
frozen over before a few times. But this time it seemed to affect
people differently.

Everyone was forced to walk across the river on the relatively
thin (somewhere around 6 inches thick) and uneven ice. This took
considerable time and frightened many. Quick-thinking entrepreneurs put ladders down to the ice and charged a ladder use fee.
This passage, though, was not safe and not guaranteed.

Suddenly the bridge seemed like the best idea ever. Yes, It looked
as if it was finally time for a change! An East River revolution was
about to occur, and Brooklyn and Manhattan would never be the
same!

## FEARS, PHOBIAS, AND FRICTION

Fear is and will always be a barrier when it comes to persuasion. We all have fears to some extent. Some are rational, some fears are not.

For example, in America, about 1 in 10 people have a phobia (an unhealthy, often irrational, crippling fear) of some sort.

Gephyrophobia is the fear of bridges, or more accurately, the fear of crossing over bridges. It's a paralyzing, debilitating fear.

The Chesapeake Bay Bridge is widely believed to be the scariest bridge in the world. It is almost 5 miles long and close to 200 feet above the water. When it storms there, it's almost impossible to see dry land. The effect is so bad that the bridge authorities have set up a Driver Assistance Service for those temporarily incapacitated by their phobia.

One popular driving magazine recently published an article on the fear of driving across bridges. It was entitled, "When Gephyrophobia Strikes, You Still Have to Cross the Bridge." This is so true. Having a fear of something does not eliminate the thing feared or the need to get over it.

Glossophobia, or fear of public speaking, is even more common among people. Around 73% of people fear public speaking, with a good amount hitting the phobia level. Just like the fear of driving over bridges, so it is with presentations. The show must go on so you might as well get used to it.

One of the leading treatment methods for phobia is Cognitive-Be-havioral Therapy (CBT). It's one form of psychological treatment for many disorders. One of CBT's tenets is facing your fears instead of avoiding them. That's precisely the goal of CBT's exposure therapy. It involves planning exposure interventions and slowly increasing the intensity until the subject is no longer overwhelmed by the stimuli. Some have even become acclimated to the point of full recovery.

If you fear public speaking, it's best to seek help and advice. You might choose an honest friend, a respected family member, a trustworthy professional presentation coach, and possibly even a good psychologist.

But in addition to exposure therapy, one thing that I have found extremely helpful is acquiring a methodology and having a clear strategy. Fear of change is often called fear of the unknown. When you're uncertain about what you're going to say and how people will react, it raises your anxiety. As you learn more about the techniques and strategies, as you learn more about your audience, as you continue to test your strategy and hone your skills, your anxieties and stress will slowly diminish.

I mention this because we are now talking about **BARRIERS**. One major barrier I often see is the presenters themselves. A lack of trust and confidence in the presenter is often one of the biggest obstacles in persuasion, sales, or influence. It's contagious when the audience sees or senses fear, anxiety, or a lack of confidence. Soon, they will feel uneasy about you, your product, and your proposal.

So before we go on to look at possible external **BARRIERS**, I want to make mention of the one potential roadblock we all carry with us – fear of speaking in public. Confronting this fear as soon as possible will help you to move past it.

So far, we've crystallized our **CHANGES**, chosen the exact purpose, and contemplated what perception we need to manifest in the situation. We've looked at our **AUDIENCE**, studied them, and found out about their loves and hates, their preferred method of communication, their philosophical view of life, beliefs, and values.

Now a crucial and challenging step will be to try and figure out why they might not want to make the **CHANGES** we seek.

Brainstorm reasons why they might say no or resist. For some topics, this might be very easy; for others, this might be extremely difficult or even impossible. But with time, persistence, and trial and error, we can usually unearth some causes and reasons.

Why aren't they already doing the thing we are proposing?
They don't know about it?
They've tried it before, with bad results?
They're being held back by someone else?
They aren't interested?

This can be very challenging because even if we were to ask someone why they don't want to change, the reason they give us might not be the exact truth. Whether they are lying or just don't know, we can only guess. People often don't know why they want or don't want to do something.

Metathesiophobia is the irrational fear of change. It's marked by a strong desire to control the environment completely. It also makes someone extremely risk-averse. They tend to play it safe. This probably describes a lot of people that you work with and know. It may also describe you.

Some people crave change and find it exciting. Others loathe it and avoid any talk of it. In the next part, we will be talking about BRIDGES that can help carry your AUDIENCE to CHANGE.

To illustrate, here in China, there is a newly built glass-bottom footbridge for tourists. It's made with high-strength bulletproof glass. They have even done demonstrations where they try to smash through it with a sledgehammer, to no avail. So although this bridge was engineered to withstand high forces and built with top-quality materials, some people are terrified of it and have to be dragged across it kicking, crying, and screaming. Others get excited and dance around and yell. Same bridge, different reactions.

A simple one-person rope bridge spanning a mighty river a few hundred feet below might be a more familiar illustration. One person would be in heaven, while the next would be in hell.

The decision-making process in humans is a complicated thing to understand. It is affected by mood, bias, intelligence, social norms, and a host of other variables. The fields of neuromarketing and advertising are all about discovering what makes people choose one thing over another and why they don't sometimes choose at all.

We can take a cue from that as we are running our presentations. Basically, presentations are like advertising in many ways. We have a message and an audience. We want to move our audience to some action. Marketing and advertising are all about selling ideas, products or services. But in presentations, we often sell an idea or concept, a project, mindset, a behavioral change, etc.

Sometimes our first thought is about the benefits our presentations will bring. This, in itself, isn't bad. But you will soon see that there are many different things to consider when trying to move someone to change.

One of those things is the BARRIERS to change.

Why might my audience not change?
Why haven't they changed already?
What do I know about them that might help shed light on their decision-making process?
What type of ideas and concepts do they usually accept?
What things do they usually disagree with or avoid?

There are many possibilities, and sometimes we will be left just guessing, experimenting, or putting clues together. But with each step, we will get closer to unearthing insights into their psyche.

There are many different aspects we can look into, but I've arranged four categories that you can brainstorm to start to get closer to the truth. This is not an exhaustive list. This list is designed to help you start asking some questions that can unearth possible roadblocks or potentially negative aspects to navigate.

All of these barriers are centralized around a common theme. This is called friction. Friction is the term used for things that cause trouble, burden, worry, concern, etc. Generally speaking, the brain tends to avoid friction and often opts to take the path of least resistance.

We will now consider 4 common areas that cause friction. They are personal, professional, physical, and psychological. You can use the following as a reference.

## PERSONAL
These are the many aspects of a person that are unique to that individual. These personal traits and attributes shape and affect the way they make their decisions and judgments. Some of these might be subconscious. The person might not even be aware of it or deny it.

### AGE
Baby Boomers, Generation X, Millennials, and Generation Z have different reference points, experience, and exposure, shaping how they think and perceive things. While these can be stereotypical and do not represent each individual, there will likely be some noticeable differences.

Are they old school or new school thinking?
What are their values, morals, and ethics?
What is their viewpoint and competence regarding technology?
What era are they from, and how might this affect their viewpoints and decisions?
How might their physical abilities affect your presentation regarding things like sound, language, and vision?

### ATTITUDE
What observations might help you gauge how they feel about you or your topic?
When are they in the best mood?
Are they apathetic to your cause?

### CULTURE
Is this presentation given in their native language? Is the language an issue?
Have you looked into their cultural background?
Sometimes people distance themselves from their surrounding culture and others are very deep into it. Ask, observe, discern.

## TRUST

Why might they feel they can't trust you?

Have you asked them their feelings beforehand on the topic?

Have they had a bad experience?

Could some seemingly unrelated things be preventing them from fully trusting you?

Could your appearance, speech, style, humor, or other factors affect their subconscious feelings toward you?

## KNOWLEDGE AND EXPERIENCE

What type and style of education did they receive?

How has this affected the way they think and reason?

Do they understand the technical parts of their work in addition to the business aspects of it?

Have they been in this industry/role long enough to grasp core concepts?

Have they ever dealt with the potential problems and issues your presentation seeks to solve?

Have they tried alternatives?

## FEAR OF CHANGE

It's often tempting for many people to stay where they are when uncertain.

Are they open to change if you prove that your idea is better?

Are they too comfortable to consider change? Status quo is the devil you know.

## INTERESTS

Have they asked you to speak about this topic or have others chosen it?

Is there a void that your topic is filling?

Is your topic relevant to their everyday work?

Does your topic provide a solution to their problems?

Do they recognize that they have a problem in the first place?

## KNOWLEDGE

Often, a gap in understanding, experience, or information can lead to a no due to the embarrassment of asking for clarity.

Are there terms, concepts, or principles they might not know?

Do they know a lot about your topic?

Will they understand the terminology or jargon you use?

Do you need to give them some background context or basic understanding of the concepts?

## LANGUAGE

Could there be misunderstandings if you are speaking in a foreign or second language?

Have you reduced any jargon, highly technical industry words, or acronyms that might obscure the meaning of your words?

## LIKES AND DISLIKES

What are their personal preferences and tastes in business and everyday life?

What fundamental things do they stand for?

Is there anything in your presentation that might trigger negative feelings about your topic?

## MOOD

Are they a morning person?

What recent events in their life might affect their decision making?

If you quickly perceive that some mood issues could negatively sway the decision-maker, look for ways to change the vibe, have the meeting but hold the pitch, or defer to another time.

## PERSONALITY
Yes, this is a big one, especially if their personality clashes with yours. Be on the lookout for any negative or neurotic traits.

Are they stubborn? Skeptical? A know-it-all? Corrupt? Lazy? Disinterested? Dismissive? Pessimistic? Condescending?
How will that affect their judgments and decision-making?

Also, this is an excellent time to decide whether you still want to work with/for this person.

## PAST EXPERIENCE
Perhaps they've tried this already or know of others who have had a bad experience with something they relate to your topic.

Are they familiar with your topic?
Have they tried something similar before?

## POSITION
Where they feel they are up the chain or not might cause them to have either overconfidence or a lack thereof.  Location, location, location.

What is their role?
Do they have a lot of authority?
Where are they in the organizational hierarchy?
What is their social status in life?
Are they in a position to confidently make a favorable decision, or are they a gatekeeper who is more likely to shoot down ideas?
Do they have a clear stake in the outcome?
What is their relationship with you?

## PREJUDICE AND PRECONCEPTIONS
It's not fair and it's not cool, but it still exists.

Is it possible that your audience has preconceived ideas about your topic?
Have they heard rumors or negative information?
I'm not sure if you noticed, but sadly, in the 21st century prejudice is still a thing.
What are their feelings about you and your background?
Do you sense any hesitation, resentment, or a standoffishness?
Is gender an issue with them?
Do you feel that they respect you and your culture?
Are there fundamental differences in preferences, tone, behavior, and communication style that may lead to misunderstandings?
Is this person in competition with you?

## COMMUNICATION STYLE
Your presentation style, whether it's the slide deck you create, your delivery, or your choice of language and tone, will affect their reaction.

What type of presentations are they used to?
Is familiar good for them, or do you need to shake them up?
Do they prefer a facts-in-the-front delivery, or are they more contextual, needing the peripheral details?

## VALUES AND IDEALS
What are their dealbreakers regarding how business should be done?
What buzzwords have they used that might clue you into what they really care about and hate?
Does your topic have any hidden mines you need to sweep for?

## PROFESSIONAL

Nothing personal, just business. These are factors that are purely business related and not unique to that individual. Professional reasons are often out of the decision-maker's control or are common to all people in that field or environment, or position, such as company policy.

### POSITION AND AUTHORITY

Are they in a position to decide?
Is there pressure on them from superiors regarding their decisions? Also, do they view you as an authority on the topic?

### CONFLICT OF INTEREST

Are your goals aligned or are you working against each other?
Are your company values in alignment?

### CULTURE

The tip of the cultural iceberg consists of the actions, judgments, and behaviors you see. The underlying value system is what drives these. This can be country or company culture and may even vary from branch to branch.

Are there standard practices and traditions you should observe?
Have you done your due diligence in researching that culture?

### FINANCIAL

Do they have the budget to afford your offer?
Is there friction in the buying process?
Are the price and value clear to them?
Do you have the data and numbers they need to see?

**INFORMATION**
Do they have adequate information to realize it's an issue, under-stand the benefits and consequences, and make a decision? Conversely, have you given them too much information, and are they possibly overwhelmed to the point of analysis paralysis?

## Status quo
## *is the devil*
## you know

**LEGALITIES** Are you working in another state or country with different laws or ethics? Is the proposal or channel you use consid-ered ethical, fair, and legal locally?

**MANPOWER** What is their situation regarding available staff? Does your project require assistance from an individual or team?**ALTERNATIVES**
Are there other options available competing with yours? Are they cheaper, easier, faster, or just better?

## RELEVANCE
This question should be obvious but is your product, idea, or service something truly of value to them?

## RISK AVERSION
Cost risk analysis is often calculated by the organization.
Would they feel like they're taking a chance?
Would it be worth it for them?

## TIMELINE
Does your proposal fit into their timeline as far as time of delivery?
Is there enough lead time?
Do they have deadlines?

## PHYSICAL
Many tangible things about us or our presentation can affect an
audience's judgment and decision-making.

Something as simple as someone's appearance can make or break
a first impression. And it's not always in a way that you might think.

## APPEARANCE
Dress and grooming, attention to detail, and style all can influence
others' impressions of us. Even physical characteristics can affect
the way we are perceived.

For example, in Behavioral Economics, there is a professor at Duke
University, Dan Ariely. He is a regular lecturer and speaker and has
also done many TED and Google talks. He has half a beard. On the
left side, he has a beard. On the right side, he is often clean-shaven.

Every time he speaks, he starts his presentation the same way. "I
didn't wake up late, and I didn't lose a bet. This isn't a fashion
statement. When I was young, I was standing next to an explosion
that burned half of my face, so I can't grow a beard on this side.
Now that you know that, you can focus on what I'm saying instead
of wondering why I have half a beard." He understands the positive
and negative power of appearances. On a side note, I still don't
understand why he doesn't shave the other side, but I digress.

What is the dress standard in the culture, country, or company that
you are presenting?
Have you observed how others dress at an event?

Usually, presenters dress slightly better than the crowd they are addressing. Yet, others don't because this can work in different ways psychologically.

For example, there is a phenomenon called the Red Sneaker Effect. A Harvard study observed that people who broke social conventions or rules were perceived to be of higher status. This has been observed in the likes of Mark Zuckerberg wearing a hoodie to board meetings or Steve Jobs' ever-present New Balance sneakers, black turtleneck, and jeans. So there is precedent for this effect, but it depends on many things. If it's obvious that you know the traditions, yet you are boldly breaking them, you might be viewed as high status. But if it's perceived by others to be accidental, coincidental, or just due to poor taste, then your competence, discernment, and intelligence could be called into question. It's slippery ground, so tread cautiously.

There is another relevant bias called the Halo Effect. It's when someone perceives a good quality or trait in someone else and then assumes that they also have other good qualities. This could be a skill, ability, appearance, or personality trait. So if someone perceives your "red sneakers" to be a brave move, they may attribute other positive qualities to you as well. But this can also be reversed. If they perceive a negative trait, they may feel you have many other negative characteristics. This is called the Horn (as in devil's) Effect.

## ATTENTION
If we appear to not care for the audience, they will, in turn, not care for us. Things such as lack of eye contact, a condescending tone of voice, closed body language, turning your back to the audience as you read the PowerPoint slides, etc., can all adversely affect their impression of you.

## CREDIBILITY
Your audience will judge you on your appearance, voice, and speaking style. For example, a softspoken person may not appear to be confident. People with a nervous tic or the fidgets will appear unsure of themselves and not confident.

"If people are failing, they look inept. If people are succeeding, they look strong and good and competent. That's the 'halo effect.' Your first impression of a thing sets up your subsequent beliefs. If the company looks inept to you, you may assume everything else they do is inept." – Daniel Kahneman, Nobel Prize winner in Economics

## DISTRACTIONS
From a baby crying to a party in the next room, I've experienced them all. It's impossible to predict or prevent them. Have you checked beforehand to see if nearby rooms have events? Can you ask to move or change the times? Simple things like asking people to silence their phones can keep the flow of the presentation going smoothly.

## TECHNOLOGY
Tech failures, lost files, overuse of features such as animation in PowerPoint, and overusing a laser pointer. (I once saw a presenter use one, and the button was stuck on. As he gestured, I watched the whole audience follow the laser on the ceiling like cats.) Technology can be an attraction that quickly turns into a distraction. Keep it simple.

## ENVIRONMENT

Have you ever been stuck in a hot elevator or outside in the cold trying to get inside but can't?

Do you think that would affect your decision-making process?

Temperature is one way our environment can affect your audience. When I run training, I'm meticulous about the temperature in the room. I'm known to keep it a little cool to keep the attention and focus high.

Other environmental factors could affect our audiences.

Are they comfortable in their chairs?
Can they see everything OK?
Can they hear everything or are there distracting noises?

## TIMING

Think about the difference between talking to someone on a Monday morning, when they've just arrived at the office and are getting to their weekend stack of emails, versus a Friday late afternoon as they are about to leave the office for drinks with friends. Different times, different frames of mind. Also, think of how pitching something before lunch versus right after lunch might affect the outcome. People are in a different state.

For example, a study in 2011 discovered Israeli judges were 65 percent more lenient in their rulings at both the beginning of the day and after breaks such as lunch. Timing is important.

## PSYCHOLOGICAL

There is a psychological phenomenon called cognitive bias. Cognitive bias is an error in thinking that occurs when people are processing and interpreting information. It affects the decisions and judgments they make. The concept was first introduced in 1972 by Amos Tversky and Daniel Kahneman.

One of the fundamental understandings of this phenomenon is called heuristics. You can think of heuristics as mental shortcuts. Your brain is very good at picking up patterns. When you spot a face in the clouds, it's evidence of that pattern recognition process looking for meaning in the world. Heuristics are primarily good, but they can also be incorrect. We can sense a pattern in something, but it may not be what our minds tell us. Correlation doesn't mean causation.

We all have biases to one degree or another. And these can be the reason someone will listen to or ignore your messages. They can hinder our audience from making a preferential decision. Conversely, we can use them to sway our audience in our direction. We will talk about that part in the BRIDGES sections.

The most common example of cognitive bias is confirmation bias. We tend to gravitate to sources of information that agree with us while disregarding, discounting, or distancing ourselves from opposing viewpoints or positions. For example, this will be evident in which news sources we choose. This also will affect how we think and make judgments.

It will also be evident by how we word our search engine requests. For example searching "Wine is good for you" vs. "Wine is bad for you." We often search to find the answer we want.

These biases can affect your audience, but they can also affect you. An example is the Curse of Knowledge. This is when we incorrectly assume that everyone knows as much as we do on a given topic. We may be so deep into our work that we walk into a presentation and talk to the audience like they've also been working on our particular project or in our field for the last 20 years.

Recently I was coaching a client on her upcoming presentation. "As you can clearly see in the graph," she began confidently. The graph was a complicated tangle of lines connecting different products, sales results, and targeted consumer demographics. It resembled some of the famous convoluted PowerPoints you see when you Google "worst PowerPoint of all time."

"Hmm," I interrupted, "that may be apparent to you, but it seems very complex to me. Do you think that your audience would quickly get the inferences from this slide?"

"Umm, I'm not sure," she said. After looking at it for a minute, she said, "To tell you the truth, I would have to analyze this for about 30 minutes before I could draw an insight or make a comment on it if this was the first time I was seeing it... and I'm a data analyst!"

Her audience, in fact, did not consist of data analysts, and she quickly saw that there was absolutely no way that they could understand that graph.

Takeaway: Don't assume your audience has the same knowledge, insight, and understanding as you do. Consider where their knowledge gaps are and how you can fill them. Bottom line: If they can't understand you, it's not likely that they'll be able to agree, align, or approve.

Here are some other common biases that could affect how your message lands. This is not an exhaustive list as there are hundreds of these biases. But you should be able to start to see how they can work against you. In the BRIDGES chapters, we will show how you can utilize cognitive biases to work for your benefit.

**The Cognitive Biases That Define Us**

**CONFIRMATION BIAS**
The tendency to filter out information that doesn't line up with our preconceived beliefs, while at the same time searching for information that supports our beliefs. This is the most common bias and one that we are all guilty of at some level.

If your audience is walking in with preconceptions and a skeptical perspective, your first challenge is to change their state of mind and get them to drop their defenses and adopt an open-minded viewpoint.

**ALIEF**
An irrational, sometimes subconscious belief or feeling, often held close even in the face of accurate data and evidence. In their head they believe the truth, but in their heart they feel differently about it. Your audience might even profess to believe the opposite, but in action, they follow their subconscious feelings.

## AESTHETIC USABILITY BIAS

People tend to attribute certain qualities to a company, product, or service if its presentation has poor aesthetics. If the appearance of the presenter or presentation is poor, they will assume the product or service is also of low quality.

How do your slides look? Well designed? Professional?
How is your graphic design game?
Do you understand some color theory basics, or do you pick colors haphazardly?
Do you use the default fonts in PowerPoint or Word or professional fonts that pair well?

## BOUNDED RATIONALITY

A situation where your audience has limits on cognition, information, and time. This can cause them to settle for things that are just good enough rather than seeking ideal solutions. This is sometimes called "satisficing." It can easily occur when our audience is disinterested, distracted, tired, obsessed with price, or doesn't see the need for the change we suggest.

Does your audience see the need for a change?
Do they understand the stakes and consequences of a bad decision or even making no decision?

## DECISION FATIGUE

When faced with too many choices, people are less likely to choose at all or are likely to take the conservative safe bet or familiar choice.

There is a famous experiment known as the jam experiment. The researchers had a table at a farmer's market. They were selling fruit jams. They had two scenarios. In one, they gave people a choice between just 6 jam flavors. In the next, they offered 24 different jams. They found that when people were given too many choices (24 in this case), it often led to no choice.

Some call this analysis paralysis – a state of indecision in the light of overwhelming choices.

Like the menu with everything under the sun on it, it's hard to choose from too many options. Reducing the options will show that we did the heavy lifting of sorting and sifting through less desirable options for their benefit.

**THE HORN EFFECT**
This is the opposite of the Halo Effect. This is the effect of transferring one negative trait for another in a person.

For example: He is unkempt and slovenly. He must not be too bright either. He can't spell well. He is probably not intelligent. Our appearance, speaking style, grammar, pronunciation, accent, visuals, logic, organizational skills, etc., will lay the basis on which people judge us. The brain will link negative perceptions of us with potential negative traits. There are some things that we can't help, such as our natural beauty, but most things can be improved and optimized.

## HYPERBOLIC DISCOUNTING
The belief that things that have an immediate effect are more important than things with an effect far in the future. Some examples are smoking even though you know eventually it will bring bad health, eating a poor diet knowing that sometime in the future you will gain weight, and buying something on credit because you know you can pay later over time.

This is somewhat linked to the Ostrich Effect, which is deliberately ignoring potential risks or problems. It's the ignorance is bliss type mentality.

Your audience may be the type to procrastinate big decisions due to indecisiveness, stress aversion, or an overly optimistic yet naive view of the future. They may need to be grounded in reality and shown the real-world consequences of poor decisions. This can often be done through case studies and storytelling, sharing examples where people just like them got into trouble by avoiding timely action.

## SUNK COST FALLACY
The tendency to continue a negative action or direction due to an earlier investment of time, money, effort, resources, etc. For example, finishing a meal/movie/book/concert you dislike just because you already paid for it.

Or consider a company that has spent a lot of time, money, and training on utilizing a particular software platform. Over the years, this system is becoming antiquated and won't integrate with modern platforms. But because they already have put so much time and money into it, they continue fighting compatibility issues and try to create painful, time-consuming workarounds instead of looking into a modern platform.

Sometimes you need to paint a picture of the future in concrete terms to show them where they will be in the future and where they will be in relation to those who have adopted your proposal.

## SURVIVORSHIP BIAS

The belief that something that has endured for a long time or through a difficult period must be true and good, while ignoring other examples to the contrary. For example, a 102-year-old man says the secret to a long life is whiskey and cigarettes. Even though he isn't a medical professional, and there are countless cases of people dying young from those things, the man believes it with all his heart. His son might point to him as an example and tell others that smoking and drinking have no adverse health effects because his dad had been indulging for most of his life and is still alive at 102.

I often run into this bias here in China. Many times a legacy company that has been around for a long time in the USA, where the headquarters is located, will feel that if a process or method has been working for decades in the USA, it will indeed work here too. Arguing with them doesn't work, but often telling a simple failure story of an equally large and successful company that tried to enter the Chinese market using the same playbook will open their minds to at least question their stance. So there is a need to show that there are scores of examples from other companies to the contrary. A good case study can be very powerful.

## ZERO SUM BIAS

A belief that one has to lose if another is to win. This can lead to escalated feelings of competition and kill any chances of a win-win solution. This can be especially hard in negotiation-type interactions. Finding a mutually beneficial deal can be very hard if our audience is set on getting the best of us.

In sales, it's important that your audience doesn't feel that you are just out to get their money. If so, they may start to treat you as the enemy. Our audience needs to feel we are on their side, not against their success.

## AMBIGUITY EFFECT

The tendency to avoid options where there is missing or incomplete information. This builds an uncomfortable feeling of uncertainty and results in an unclear measure of how success looks.

Your audience has to be able to envision your product, service, or proposal. Comprehension is critical for future visualization. Good audience research and initial interaction with them will make sure that you lay the groundwork for understanding. Comprehension checks at each new phase of your message will further ascertain if they are following you or not.

## FUNCTIONAL FIXEDNESS (MASLOW'S HAMMER)

The tendency to see things as used one way or being limited to one application. This limits your audience to viewing a product, service, or concept only in how it is traditionally used or applied.

Once again, practical case studies and examples that show innovative alternatives and how they were successful will help them to abandon their one-way thinking.

## HOT HAND FALLACY

The hot-hand fallacy, or phenomenon, is the false belief that a person who has experienced success has a greater chance of further success in the following attempts.

This could be a one-hit wonder company feeling that since their one product went viral, the next one will too.

Your audience will have to be able to look at their successes, as well as their failures, objectively. They may need to see the precarious position they are in more accurately.

## REACTANCE (BACKFIRE EFFECT)

In psychology, the urge to do the opposite of what someone wants you to do out of a need to resist a perceived attempt to constrain your freedom of choice.

It's not just teenage rebellion. Adults do it too. Most people will push back when there is a feeling of limiting options or forcing their hand. Your audience needs to feel that they are in control of their decisions and aren't being coerced or manipulated. If you can get them to come up with the solution by carefully guiding them, they will be more likely to accept and follow up on that decision.

And one final note of importance. Often one of the biggest barriers is you. I often see that my clients are aware of any or all of the above points we covered but are too stubborn or attached to what they want to tell the audience that they won't change to fit their audience. CHANGE has to start with you!

So as you move on through this book, please pause to try to adopt the mindset to adapt to, and navigate around these common BARRIERS.

Takeaways

- Your first barrier may be in your mind: fear of public speaking. Resolutely decide to overcome this fear.

- People tend to avoid friction (resistance) and will most often choose the path of least resistance.

- There are four major types of BARRIERS to consider

- PERSONAL: Things unique to an individual

- PROFESSIONAL: Aspects generally accepted by a culture, company, or country

- PHYSICAL: The environment, aesthetics, experience, or appearance of a presenter.

- PSYCHOLOGICAL: Cognitive bias and emotional filters.

# BRIDGES: OVER
## TROUBLED WATERS

**"Poetry has never been the language of barriers, it's always been the language of bridges."**

**Amanda Gorman**

After 14 years of blood, sweat, and tears, working in grueling conditions, the bridge was finally completed!

On May 24, 1883, under a moonlit sky, 14 tons of fireworks were being set off to commemorate the event. It had been a festive day, full of speeches, music, revelry, and even a large parade.

The first one to cross the bridge was, of course, Emily. She went across in a carriage holding a rooster, which symbolized victory. And a victory it was. It was being called the eighth wonder of the world and had broken all records as the longest suspension bridge at the time. It was over 50% longer than all others!

More than 1,800 cars and 150,000 pedestrians crossed the bridge that day! They wondered at its stately grandeur. Yet an interesting line in the *Brooklyn Eagle* newspaper article that day was both retrospective and foreshadowing. "To every human undertaking, there seems of necessity to be a dark side." Official numbers vary, but estimates say anywhere from 21 to 40 people died during the project's construction, with hundreds of others severely wounded.

"Had we thought so many would have been injured, we would have kept a list, but we never imagined anyone would be hurt or that the bridge would have occupied so long a time in building," said C.C. Martin, first assistant engineer.

But opening day went smoothly, and it appeared that all that was in the past now. Yet six days later on Memorial Day weekend, on May 30, 1883, a crowd of people numbering about 15,000-20,000 were crossing the bridge. Due to that sunny day's large numbers, everything bottlenecked for the pedestrians at a narrow wooden stairwell on the Manhattan side. People were pressing against one another, and suddenly, a woman tripped and fell down the stairs.

"As she lost her footing, another woman screamed. Panic. Suddenly the throng behind crowded forward so rapidly that those at the top of the steps were pushed over and fell in a heap," said *The New York Times*. "Those following were in turn pushed over and in a moment the narrow stairway was choked with human beings, piled one on top of the other, who were being crushed to death. In a few minutes, 12 persons were killed, 7 injured so seriously that their lives are despaired of, and 28 others more or less severely wounded."

Deep-seated fears had unexpectedly come to the surface. People still had trust issues with the bridge. The stampede had further eroded this trust.

But the real question would be... could it be won back?

How do you gain back the people's trust? Do you share the equations and architectural formulas that prove the bridge was strong enough? In fact, the bridge was calculated to be 6X as strong as needed. Yet despite these facts, distrust remained. What could be done?

Earlier, long before the opening day, P.T. Barnum, legendary circus owner, offered to have some of his elephants walk across the bridge as evidence of its immense strength. His offer was turned down. But now, in the face of public distrust, something else was needed. The numbers had been shared and the proof given. But they would need something that would appeal, not just to logic, but to their underlying emotional trust issues.

So on May 17, 1884, P.T. Barnum had his chance to do just that. As *The New York Times* reported on the story, "At 9:30, 21 elephants, 7 camels, and 10 dromedaries issued from the ferry at the foot of Courtlandt Street... The other elephants shuffled along, raising their trunks and snorting as every train went by. Old Jumbo brought up the rear." (Old Jumbo was a large African elephant, the pride and joy of the circus.) The article also noted that "To people who looked up from the river at the big arch of electric lights it seemed as if Noah's Ark were emptying itself over on Long Island."

Yes, this visible demonstration of strength was just what the people needed to tip the scales of trust towards the bridge.

# TRUST OR BUST

The way you gain trust is not just logical – it's psychological.

People need to feel something before they change. It could be recalling something from a past memory, remembering what someone told them long ago, an emotional epiphany, a eureka revelation!

When there are lingering doubts or negative feelings, it's very hard to change minds. What if your audience doesn't trust the validity of your message, the source of your facts, the accuracy of your predictions. What if they just don't trust you?

Is it possible to change the way someone feels about you?

**The subtle art of disrobing in public**
In the last chapter, we discussed potential barriers to making the change we desire.

One question I've been asked before many times is "What do you do if someone doesn't like you?" The colleague who is always criticizing you. The boss who has it in for you. The client who seems to distrust everyone including you. If they don't like you, they will not let themselves be persuaded by you.

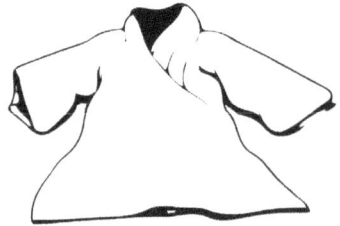

"What do you do if someone doesn't like you?" It's a great question. And it's a great name for a TED Talk. A few years ago, a man named Daryl Davis gave just that TED talk with just that title.

Daryl Davis is a tall, heavyset gentleman with a large frame and rotund figure. He has a comforting, familiar style of speaking and a kind demeanor. He speaks with a deep calm voice and the slightest twinge of southern drawl. He's a gentle giant.

He's an accomplished keyboardist and can play fluently in a variety of styles, from blues to jazz to rock. He has natural timing, a great ear for melody, and a knack for rhythm.

He is also black. The reason that is significant is because of the cause he has taken upon himself.

Daryl was born in Chicago. He was bright, optimistic, and curious as a child. He joined the Boy Scouts and loved to go on outings and marches.

On one such march in the streets of his town, he experienced something that would stay with him forever. As he proudly marched down the street, he suddenly felt something hard hit him. He soon noticed a barrage of objects coming his way. "Why would people be hurling things at us?" he thought. But soon, he realized that he was the only target in the group. The other boys were not in any danger. His teachers quickly ran over, shielded him, and bundled him away to safety.

As his parents treated his fresh wounds, they told him something that he would never forget. They explained to him that he was different because he was black. Some people would not like him because of that.

"How can someone not like me if they don't even know me?" he thought. He was right, of course, to think that and expect and deserve fair treatment. Yet, over and over again he would see this type of hatred rear its ugly head in one place after another. How can someone hate me if they don't even know me? This question would haunt him as, time and time again, racism, sometimes subtle, oftentimes undisguised, would reappear.

On one such occasion, he realized his calling. He had a gig with his band at a honky-tonk bar down South. He was the only black man in the band. Everyone in the bar was white. After playing a vigorous set and drawing much applause, he sat at the bar to grab a drink.

An older man walked up and told him he liked his playing. "I've never seen a black man play honky-tonk like Jerry Lee Lewis before!" he excitedly said. Daryl tried to explain that Jerry Lee Lewis' style came from the blues-rock of the time, created and perfected by black musicians. And Jerry Lee Lewis had "borrowed" it, much the same as Elvis had borrowed from the black blues musicians before him. "Nah, that can't be true. I never heard of those guys," the man said incredulously. Daryl actually knew Jerry Lee Lewis personally and was friends with him! Yet Daryl let it go and continued the conversation and shared a few drinks.

A little later, the man abruptly and unabashedly announced, "You know, this is the first time I've ever had a drink with a black man." Daryl was surprised. Daryl had traveled extensively and had held hundreds if not thousands of conversations with other men that were white.

Next to the man stood another friend. "Tell him," the friend said.
"Tell me what?" Daryl asked.
"Well," the man paused. "Well, I'm a member of the KKK."
Daryl laughed in disbelief. "That's funny," he said.

"No really, I am," the man quickly said. He then reached into his wallet and pulled out his KKK membership card to prove it. Daryl stopped laughing. A deeper conversation ensued and right then and there, Daryl was determined to finally find the answer to his question.

How can someone hate me if they don't even know me? The question had continued to ring in his ears for so long, that he could no longer stand it. He finally vowed to get the answer. Daryl went on to seek out Klansmen and interview them.

He decided to just ask questions and not argue with them. It wasn't easy. They would spew out many ignorant theories about how black people were inferior in one way or another. Obviously, they had no backing to these claims, but Daryl never asked them for it. He just asked questions and listened respectfully to their answers. After a while, he found these men dropping their offensive, lowering their defenses, and eventually retiring their hateful rhetoric. They started to warm up to him and soon adopted a silent respect for him. They felt listened to. They felt the fear of the unknown subside.

One by one, Daryl slowly won them over with his calm, cool, and compassionate personality. They began to trust him, open up to him, and eventually even like him. They would invite him to their Klan rallies, and Daryl would accept. He would often stand in the front or even have backstage access as a distinguished guest.

Eventually, without his even prodding, they would realize that they had gone down the wrong path. One after another, they renounced their membership and moved away from their former brethren.

His involvement with these men has resulted in well over 200 Klansmen turning in their membership cards and retiring their robes. Many have sent their robes to him as a souvenir and proof of their transition from hate. When asked how he persuaded them, he says he just listened, and they converted themselves.

If someone doesn't like you, it's most likely because they don't really know you. If you are ever faced with a person in your workplace that doesn't seem to like you, perhaps they even hate you, please remember the powerfully persuasive method that Daryl Davis used on those men through asking and listening. A remarkable man, a fantastic story, and an amazing lesson for us all.

I'm not saying that everyone in the world will like you or that you can persuade anyone to do anything. I'm just saying that people have overcome incredible odds in the past, and Daryl's story proves that there's no barrier that can't be overcome.

It also shows the immense power of questions. Questions, when deftly wielded, are more often than not, more powerful than statements. You will notice I use questions as prompts in this book a lot. Often statements trigger reactance. Questions can often plant a seed where statements take no root. Why is this? It's all psychology.

The way you gain **trust** is not just **logical** it's *psychological*

**Different strokes for different folks**
As we looked at earlier, there are many different kinds of people with different personalities, backgrounds, opinions, philosophies, etc. Therefore we must look at each persuasion attempt differently as well. Just as we would use different tools for different jobs, so we would also choose our methods based on the unique challenges ahead.

# Questions can often plant a seed where statements take no root

In this chapter, we will look at some techniques we could use. This is not an exhaustive list and it's not intended to be. There are a million different tactics with an equal amount of applications. The goal is to go through the CHANGE, AUDIENCE, and BARRIERS and then select the best BRIDGES for the job. This will involve experimenting a bit to get a feel for each technique. Learning which ones work well together for different people on different occasions is a skill that takes time, experimentation, and practice.

Let's consider a few different options and aspects of persuasive communication and how they can be implemented.

There are many common ways to do this, like using facts, logic, numbers, graphs, and charts.

Then there are next-level skills like using humor, storytelling, illustrations, and rhetoric. Using Aristotle's 3 modes of Ethos, Pathos, and Logos. And there are many books on those topics.

We will focus on some applied Behavioral Economics principles and how you can use them to optimize your presentation for persuasiveness.

Firstly, I would be remiss if I didn't mention the unique power of storytelling. A strategic story is a mental and emotional shortcut that attracts and focuses our attention, conveys information in a relatable way, and connects and interacts with past memories, stimulating our emotions. Remember – emotions help us make decisions.

I will cover this more in the last chapter and even more in-depth in another future book. Stay tuned. As we go through these last chapters, we will cover many principles and emotional triggers that can move your audience to change.

You can use these principles inside of stories. Once you pick a principle or principles that could be used for persuasion, try to find a story that utilizes those principles and tease out details and aspects that optimize them. I'll touch more on stories in the last chapter of this book.

## Words matter: The nuances of Nudges
Here are a few Behavioral Economics principles that we can apply to our persuasive communication interventions.

### PRIMING AND FRAMING
Priming and framing are similar in effect yet slightly different in definition.

Priming, or the Priming Effect, is the positive or negative effect of a first stimulus on processing a second stimulus that appears shortly after. In other words, by exposing someone to a word, sound, smell, image, etc., you can get them to associate it with a thought, memory, or feeling. This can affect how they view the next thing they think of, hear, or see.

Framing, or the Framing Effect, is a cognitive bias where people decide on options based on whether the options are presented positively or negatively, as a loss or a gain.

Priming is done right before new information is given, in order to change how that information is received, while framing relates to how information is shared. It can be shared with a positive or negative spin. Often these effects overlap a bit, and both effects take place simultaneously.

For example, in one famous experiment, researchers showed participants a short video of a car crash. They then asked them to guess the speed of the car before the crash. For some, they asked how fast they thought the car was traveling before it "bumped" the other car. For others, they used the word "slammed" instead of "bumped."

By changing the verb intensity, they found that people would guess in the direction of the verb. In the results, "bumped" got lower speed guesses, and "slammed" had higher ones.

Words matter. Here is another example.

Researchers Lera Boroditsky and Paul Thibodeau ran some experiments on the effect of metaphors.

They asked 1,482 students to read a report about crime in a fictional city. Then the students were asked to choose solutions for handling the crime problem.

But there was a catch. There were two different reports. Half of the group got one version, and the other half received a different one. Both reports were identical except for one word.

The first report said that crime in the city was like A) a beast, and the second said it was like B) a virus.

In A) crime is like a beast, 75% of the participants chose reactive solutions involving enforcement or punishment. Only 25% suggested social reforms such as fixing the economy, improving education, or providing better health care.

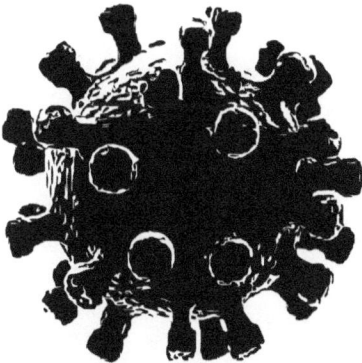

In B) crime is like a virus, the participants' solutions were more proactive. Only 56% chose more enforcement, while 44% suggested social reforms.

The metaphors influenced how the participants saw the problems and how they thought about solving them.

What's more, after the experiment, they were asked to circle the parts of the text that they thought influenced them. Only 3% circled the metaphors. The rest circled the statistics and numbers. They didn't realize or couldn't accept that the metaphors had any influence. Yet the repeated results overwhelmingly concluded that they had.

Additionally, the researchers found that these metaphors only worked if they were mentioned before the rest of the information was given. If they were mentioned at the end, they had no significant effect.

The team has continued to study language's powerful effects, particularly metaphors, on people's judgment and decision making.

Further study involved the use of other metaphors. One common one they looked at was the war metaphor: the war on drugs, the war against cancer, even the war against climate change, for example.

This metaphor seemed to inform the different actions that groups would take. For example, the war on drugs. Government agencies like the DEA took on a more military feel. They would often describe actions in battle-like language. They would use strategic terms akin to military strikes. They started to dress like an army with tactical clothing and masked faces. And they eventually armed themselves like actual soldiers.

When these government agencies would update their arsenal, their old equipment was often handed down to local police agencies – the uniforms, the protective gear, the armored military vehicles, the assault weapons. What effect would this have on the police departments?

Thibodeau was curious about this and wanted to find out. He wondered about how even the metaphor a police department chose to describe themselves would affect their actions. Some had been calling themselves guardians, others warriors.

The Obama administration also realized this at the time and put out a report addressing this difference. It read: "Law enforcement culture should embrace a guardian – rather than a warrior – mindset to build trust and legitimacy both within agencies and with the public."

Yes, studies found that choosing to use the term guardian led officers to take on a more proactive outlook to crime and the people they were protecting, while the term warrior gave the officers a more aggressive and reactive mindset.

In a more recent study, Yale psychology professor John Barth and his team found that by simply framing a conversation with certain interventions, they could sway people's ideals and beliefs. In his book, *Before You Know It: The Unconscious Reasons We Do What We Do,* he writes, "Research has shown that you can make liberals more conservative by threatening them and making them somewhat afraid." The opposite, it turns out, also works.

The experiment he ran involved researchers telling a group of participants to imagine that a genie had granted them a superpower: they would be invincible like Superman. They could fly. They would be bulletproof, fireproof, and generally unbreakable. The study's control group, on the other hand, was just told to imagine they could fly.

Then the researchers asked the participants to give their opinions on some political statements, including whether they "would be reluctant to make any large-scale changes to the social order," and whether "it's OK if some groups have more of a chance in life than others."

Liberal participants' attitudes on social issues didn't change at all. The conservative participants, on the other hand, started adopting more liberal views on social issues.

Participants who imagined themselves with only the ability to fly had no change in their political views. The study authors say this is some of the first experimental evidence that making people feel completely safe can change their politics and make them more liberal. It should be noted that this was only a temporary change while they were in this imaginative state.

So what can we learn from these experiments? Words matter. Choose the way you frame your arguments carefully.

Choose words with positive connotations for things you want to promote and negative ones for those you want to discourage. A word of caution, be careful about using words that are over the top or too exaggerative. You don't want to lose credibility by sounding unreasonable or illogical. The key is to drizzle your language with persuasiveness, not drench it!

## ANCHORING
The Anchoring Effect is a cognitive bias where an individual's decisions are influenced by the introduction of a reference point, or anchor. We are disproportionally influenced by the first piece of information we hear. Once the anchor is deployed, arguments, estimates, or any other information may change from what they would have otherwise been without the anchor.

For example, Tversky and Kahneman ran an experiment where they had high school students guess the answers to mathematical equations in a very short period of time. They were only given 5 seconds to estimate the answer. You can try it now too. What's your guess?

A/  $8 \times 7 \times 6 \times 5 \times 4 \times 3 \times 2 \times 1 = ?$

Another group was given the same sequence, but in reverse:

B/  $1 \times 2 \times 3 \times 4 \times 5 \times 6 \times 7 \times 8 = ?$

In A/ the average guess was 2,250. In B/ it was 512.

The correct answer is 40,320. But notice the vast contrast in answers. Giving the higher number first anchors the listeners' perspective, and thus their conclusions.

Side note: In pricing strategy, many use a bracketing system. This is where you give a range of possible prices, such as "This will cost anywhere from $500 to $3,000." An effective tweak on this is reversing the order to anchor your client to the higher number. Such as: "This will cost anywhere from $3,000 down to $500." They will naturally feel better paying anything under the $3,000 anchor.

This effect also occurs with word order. For example, Solomon Asch ran some experiments where participants heard a string of words describing someone and had to make judgments about them.

Intelligent. Industrious. Impulsive. Critical. Stubborn. Envious.

Another group heard the same list, but in reverse.

Envious. Stubborn. Critical. Impulsive. Industrious. Intelligent.

Even though the information is identical in content, the order it was given changed everything. Participants who were given the positive words first formed a much higher opinion than the ones who viewed the negative words first.

So think carefully about the order in which you give information. It can have a bigger effect than you may have realized.

### Befriending bias
Earlier, we discussed cognitive biases and how they can become a BARRIER for your audience. Now we'll use them as BRIDGES

As we said before, there are hundreds of them. We will be taking a look at a few common ones, and even some you may have not heard of, and see how to apply them to your next communication intervention.

## ATTENTION + FOCUS + MEMORY

By using certain biases to your advantage, you can focus your audience's attention on you, your main points, your CTA (call to action), or the option you want them to choose instead of other options.

When I do workshops, I often do this exercise with my participants. I tell them to close their eyes and I read off a list of 10 words. When I am finished, I tell them to write down all the words they remember. Here is the list:

**Dream**
Sleep
**Night**
Mattress
Sheets
Tired
**Night**
**Basketball** (I usually read this word with an exaggerated foreign accent)
Blanket
**Night**
Alarm
Nap
Snore
**Pillow**

The words in bold are usually the ones remembered. Why? I'll explain why as we go through the different biases next.

Here are the ones most often remembered and the corresponding effect. I'll explain the effect in more detail in the next few pages.

**Dream** and **pillow** are remembered due to the Primacy-Recency Effect. People remember the first and last thing they hear or see. **Night** is remembered due to the Attentional Bias Effect. By repeating it 3X, the message is reinforced. **Basketball** is remembered due to the Von Restorff Effect. Things that are different or novel get remembered.

People frequently remember the word "bed" even though I never said it. So sometimes we can evoke a word or idea without saying it. This can come in handy if we want to get our audience to think about something without actually saying it ourselves. Remember this point when you read about the IKEA Effect later in this chapter, as well as the storytelling section.

# The key is to drizzle your message with persuasion Not drench it!

## ATTENTIONAL BIAS (SALIENCE)

The tendency of our perception to be affected by repeated imagery, words, or concepts. Your audience will think about things they remember. People remember things that are regularly heard.

Repeat your main thought, message, or call to action at different points, and in different ways, in your presentation.

People will often remember "night" in the word list above because I repeat it three times! These things become top of mind: salient.

Repetition is commonly overlooked in presentations. Most people assume that it's redundant and boring to use the same words repeatedly. Yet, please think back to the last presentation that you heard and try to pick out the main points. It's not easy, is it?

In a round table documentary on comedy, comedian Chris Rock was asked why he often repeats himself. He often makes a statement, then tells a story as an example of that statement, and then afterwards repeats his initial statement a few times. Jerry Seinfeld piped in and said, "He has to do that because that's a richer idea than they're used to hearing... so he has to teach them." Chris agreed and added, "A lot of comedians have great jokes but wonder 'why is this not working?' It's because the audience doesn't understand the premise... if I set this premise up right, this joke will always work."

It's the same with your presentation's premise and punchline – the call to action. Set it up right, say it, and then repeat the premise; it'll always work! Sometimes the audience needs time and repetition to absorb your message.

Repetition, repetition, repetition!

## VON RESTORFF EFFECT (ALSO ISOLATION EFFECT)

When a list or group of things are all the same or similar, the one that contrasts or is significantly different will stand out and most likely be remembered. Memory is not only good for attention and retention, but it often can spark change.

This is why they often remember the word "basketball" in the word list above. It's different, it breaks a pattern, and I say it in a foreign accent to make it further stand out and imprint it in the memory.

When you want to emphasize a point, draw attention, or aid memory retention, try to break a pattern with something surprising, shocking, or novel. You can do this in many ways, such as changing your vocal style. You can vary your pitch, your pace, or your power. You could try adding a slide with an interesting or intriguing image that visually stimulates your audience rather than the typical cliche stock photos.

Whenever you want to get your audience's attention and focus, you need to signal to them that something special is happening right now.

## DECOY EFFECT

The Decoy Effect describes how, when choosing between two alternatives, the addition of a third, less attractive option (the decoy) can influence our perception of the original two choices.

When giving two options, you could add a third that is only there to guide your audience. For example, if you have a choice between two options, A and B, and you want them to choose A, adding another option, C, that is similar to A yet inferior, will make A stand out as the more desirable choice.

This works great for proposals where we are offering more than one option as a possibility. Also, if you are making a pricing strategy that involves three prices ranging from low to high, the middle option will likely sell the most.

**DISTINCTION BIAS**
This is the tendency to view two options as very different when evaluating them simultaneously, in contrast to evaluating them separately.

Contrast is a powerful tool when decision-making is involved. If you want to compare two things to show differences, make sure to put them side by side rather than explain one and then go on to the other.

You can use a technique made famous by presentation guru Nancy Duarte. She calls this method a "sparkline" but I call it repetitive contrast. Basically, you express what is happening or available now, and then you show your solution or paint your picture of the future, then go back to now, and then back to the future (yeah, yeah, I know, *Back to the Future*).

You can repeat this over and over again. What happens is it takes a while for the new concept to sink in and by going back and forth and repeating it, you get that side-by-side analysis and the contrast is magnified.

The more contrast you show, the more powerful the effect. Duarte first noticed this with Martin Luther King's "I have a dream" speech. He went back and forth between what was currently occurring and his future "dream" state.

Steve Jobs also displayed this technique when he first introduced the iPhone in 2007. He spoke of "so-called smart phones" and how they were better than average phones but not as easy to use. He spoke of how clunky they were when you were trying to type with the little buttons. Then he spoke of how easily the iPhone Touch could be navigated.

He spoke of how easy it was to get food and drink stuck in the keyboard when using the other phones. And then showed the sleek iPhone Touch navigated through the screen.

He spoke of how hard it was to type on the go and how two hands were required to operate the other phones. And then there was the smooth one-hand operation of the iPhone Touch. The repetitive contrast really crystallized the stark differences.

Sometimes, a side-by-side chart or checklist can work well to show the difference clearly. He showed a graph with the vertical axis showing ease of use and the horizontal showing how "smart" phones were. The graph showed all the current smartphones huddled into the edge of the screen, slightly smarter than the average phone yet at the extreme of hard to use.

Then he made a gesture of something taking off as he said, "We want to make a leapfrog product that is waaay smarter than any mobile device has ever been and is suuuper easy to use… This is what iPhone is," as a large green circle appeared in the top right quadrant of the graph – elevated and clearly superior to the others.

He then displayed a visual of the 4 major players in the smartphone game. He had the Moto Q, Blackberry, Palm Treo, and Nokia E62. He explained and contrasted one by one how the iPhone was superior to all other competitors.

Often the tendency is to list all the bad aspects of the alternatives, then list all the good aspects of our concept and say, "OK, so buy, accept, approve!" But the back and forth rhythm of using repetitive contrast gives the audience time to wrap their heads around the issue at hand and absorb the magnitude of the differences. With each repetition the gap mentally increases and the divide gets deeper. Your audience needs a little time, not only to see the difference, but to also "feel" the difference.

## RHYME AS REASON EFFECT

Rhyming statements are perceived as more truthful. A famous example comes from the OJ Simpson trial: speaking of a pair of gloves in evidence, the defense said: "If it doesn't fit, then you must acquit."

The psychological part is where our brain assumes that the mere fact of the sounds being congruent equals the sentence's logic being congruent.

You can apply this by having a tagline in your presentation that rhymes.

Similarly, alliteration, a close cousin to rhyming, is the use of an initial consonant sound repeated in a string of words. It can affect how your audiences receive and perceive your message. For example, when I spoke of Daryl Davis, I said he was "calm, cool, and compassionate." The close concentration of C's together has a ring of consistency, certainty, and correctness. (Oops, I did it again.) It just sounds concrete. Don't delay, try rhyming today!

## PICTURE SUPERIORITY EFFECT

Concepts learned by viewing pictures are more easily and frequently recalled than concepts learned by viewing their written word counterparts.

Studies show again and again that pictures are more memorable than just using the spoken word or written language. So incorporating vivid visuals into your presentations can significantly increase attention and retention. Your first impulse may be to look for interesting pictures and images online. That's not a bad idea, but is it the best idea?

A study conducted at Stanford University by Dr. Zak Tormala put three different types of communication up against each other. One was a simple PowerPoint text structure of the main point with corresponding bullet points. The next was the Zen type Power-Point slide, with an image taking up the whole slide and some text arranged over the picture. The last was a whiteboard-type visual where the words were written out in real time.

Surprisingly, the whiteboard style visual performed better than the other two by a significant margin. It had the effect of a 17% increase of recall after two days! So although PowerPoint can indeed be powerful, there is something about a live visual display that can be engaging and persuasive.

In my training, I always try to incorporate both. I will have slides to convey the concepts and then draw them on the whiteboard as a running log of things learned and discussed. It serves as a great memory aid and a visual recall tool for a summary at the end.

# Your audience

Needs a little time not only to

# see

# the difference

## but to also

# feel

# the difference

## SEQUENCING AND PLACEMENT

### PRIMACY-RECENCY EFFECT

As you may have noticed in the list above, people remember the first thing you say (primacy) and the last (recency). Therefore, it's vital to make sure that we take advantage of that effect and get our key message in those sweet spots.

Start with a hook that gets attention and intrigues the audience. You want them to be thinking, what's next? Or how can I do that?

Stories are great for building interest and intrigue. Starting with a story and then weaving that story throughout the presentation, only revealing the story's conclusion at the end, will keep attention high throughout and have people remain curious until the end.

You can pose a question or a problem that needs solving. If they pay attention, you can offer a promise or a guarantee that your presentation will fulfill.

Your conclusion should also be memorable. Usually I see a Q&A at the end and when there are no more questions, the presenter just says, "OK, well, that's all I had to say today, thanks for your time." This anticlimactic ending doesn't leave them with a clear thought in mind. Always have some closing words after the Q&A and ensure that your call to action is clear, easy to execute, and all friction is removed for the next step you want them to take.

## PEAK-END RULE

People seem to perceive and remember not the overall average point of an experience but the average of how it was at its peak (the best or worst) and how it ended. Perhaps you might think of a past relationship you had where looking back now, you remember the best times but may forget the rest. (OK, please don't think too long about that, it was just an example.)

So, therefore, you need to create and emphasize a peak moment in your presentation. Having a high point will give you a goal to work towards and a stabilizing North Star for your audience to anchor your speech on. It could be a realization, an observation, an announcement, a launch, a tagline that will reappear and be reemphasized in months to come, etc. (Think: Today, Apple is revolutionizing the phone!) The key is that it should be an emotional anchor for your audience to focus on during your presentation.

As you develop your presentation, structure in a high point that you can put somewhere in the middle that you can work towards, highlight, and then reinforce and reemphasize as you move towards your conclusion.

## PERCEPTION AND FRICTION

### HALO EFFECT
(OPPOSITE OF THE HORN EFFECT) The Halo Effect, as mentioned before, is when people see a positive trait or quality in someone and then assume that the person must have other similar traits or qualities. These qualities don't have to have a relationship to each other. For example, if you see someone who is well dressed and particular in their grooming, you may assume they are diligent and detail oriented in their work as well. This assumption could be wrong, but it's a natural tendency to use heuristics like this to make judgments and decisions.

Therefore first impressions are extremely important and difficult to erase. We can't always change our physical appearance significantly, but we can be deliberate about the perception we want to give and how we come across.

Often our first impression is not when we start our presentation, but the first time someone sees us. They may size us up and make a snap judgment before we even open our mouths. I always try to get to an event early and meet as many people as possible before a speech. Getting into the right headspace and mood before I enter the room is critical. Taking a natural, authentic interest in those you meet will solidify a good first impression which you can reinforce later in your presentation.

Likewise, others will judge your appearance, whether you think it's fair or not. So think of your audience and try to find out where their expectations are, regarding dress, grooming, and decorum.

Starting positively increases trust and likability, and will help them form a positive first impression. More on that later.

# People
## dont resist
# *change*
## they resist
### being changed

**ILLUSION OF CONTROL**
This is the tendency to overestimate our ability to measure and control our environment. We all want to have a strong measure of control over our lives; when that is threatened, we get stressed.

"People don't resist change, they resist being changed."
– Peter Senge, scientist at MIT

Give choices, give options, educate them to tell the difference between good and bad on their own so they can come to the same conclusion as you have. Giving your audience a feeling of control can be very powerful. If you can subtly lead them to a revelation or conclusion on their own, it is much more powerful and persuasive.

## PSEUDOCERTAINTY EFFECT

This is the tendency to avoid risk if your audience thinks there will be a good outcome and accept risk when they feel the outcome could be negative.

When appealing to a positive emotion and painting a picture of a bright future, it's good not to spotlight the risks involved. This could easily spook them. Conversely, if you're appealing to negative emotions such as fear, frustration, or pain points, then there may be a need to emphasize risk to put them into a state of mind where they feel that change is necessary.

If you highlight not only the negative consequences of a decision but also the ripple effect that it will have in the future, your audience is more likely to see how critical CHANGE is.

## AMBIGUITY EFFECT

People are more likely to avoid options when information about the options is missing or scarce.

One thing that often obscures clear information on options is the use of jargon or insider technical language. Acronyms, abbreviations, and tech terms can all get in the way of clear communication. People will say no when they are not sure. The answer will likely be no if they don't clearly understand.

One way to avoid ambiguity is by putting numbers into perspective. If you share a number, try to give the number context. Tell the audience what that number was last year this time, what the average is, why it's so unique or unusual for that number to be where it is now. Or tell them exactly why it's good or bad for the number to be what it is and what the real-life consequences will be if it doesn't change.

These are just a small sampling of the psychological principles you can use to optimize your message persuasively. The idea is to spend adequate time brainstorming angles that might optimize persuasion.

Takeaways

- Trust is the key enabler of persuasion.

- Utilize psychological appeals to your advantage while remaining wary of the two-edged sword potential.

- Questions, rapport building, and patience are your best bets to overcome bias and prejudice.

- Timing, sequencing, positioning, and word choice can make or break your presentation. You can pick and choose from many psychological effects to craft an effective presentation.

# BRIDGES APPLIED POP PSYCHOLOGY

**"Passion is the bridge that takes you from pain to change."**

**Frida Kahlo**

"A POEM OF GRANITE and steel" is how famed architectural critic Lewis Mumford described the Brooklyn Bridge. He wrote: "All that the age had just cause for pride in—its advances in science, its skill in handling iron, its personal heroism in the face of dangerous industrial processes, its willingness to attempt the untried and the impossible—came to a head in Brooklyn Bridge.

"The stone plays against the steel: the heavy granite in compression, the spidery steel in tension. In this structure, the architecture of the past, massive and protective, meets the architecture of the future, light, aerial, open to sunlight, an architecture of voids rather than of solids."

In the last chapter, we spoke of how P.T. Barnum demonstrated the bridge's strength by parading across 21 elephants. But there were other factors at play in the bridge's architecture. Knowing that there was so much doubt in the air, its creators designed for trust.

The aesthetics and architecture of the bridge had deliberate psychological elements in its design. The original plans made by John Roebling resembled ancient Egyptian architecture but were changed by his son Washington after his father's death.

The steel elements that make up the structural skeleton are covered in large granite stones in a neo-Gothic style reminiscent of the cathedrals and churches of Europe. This evokes familiarity and the feeling of institution – something to be trusted.

The height alone of the towers gives it a lofty presence, especially considering that it was the tallest structure in North America at the time.

The two large-pointed arches strayed from traditional neo-Gothic style and were instead crafted to resemble the windows of a church – thus inspiring sacredness and holiness. Many have noticed the resemblance of the twin arches to two sets of praying hands. It truly is a sprawling fortress offering safe passage to all who require it.

S UASIVE = SAFE, SOUND, **and secure**

The bridge has seen its share of times when safe passage was indeed required. I'll never forget September 11, 2001. It was called Big Tuesday because a massive swell was hitting the nearby beaches. The day promised the best surfing of the year.

I had just left Brooklyn Heights and was headed for the most epic surf of the year on Long Island. As I came to one of the bridges, the toll booth attendant asked us if we had heard that a plane hit one of the twin towers. "What kind of plane?" I asked. "I don't know, a Cessna maybe," he replied. "How many were hurt?" I asked ."I'm not sure, but I'm sure the pilot's not doing so well," he replied.

After I had been surfing for a while, someone came out and said they heard it was a commercial airliner and that it was terrorism. "No way," we thought, "that can't be." Half an hour later, we heard of the second tower being hit, then the Pentagon, and of course, of the devastating collapses.

It took me hours to make the usually short drive back to Brooklyn Heights. All the traffic lights were in emergency mode.

As I got back to Brooklyn Heights I'll never forget seeing the hordes of people walking across the bridge, looking for somewhere to wash up, seek medical attention, and get help.

The next day two friends and I hitched a ride with a nurse across the Brooklyn Bridge. The National Guard had arrived and only military, governmental, and medical personnel were allowed across. We wanted to help.

After helping with the search and rescue work for the day, we walked back across the now grey, ash-covered bridge, slowly and pensively. So when I say there's nostalgia and sentimentality between the bridge and I, I mean it. The bridge is a vision of safety and security.

**POP culture: The Principles Of Persuasion**

Likewise, your presentations should always be designed with your audience's perceptions of safety and security in mind. There is always a risk involved in trusting someone. Your audience might be putting their money, time, energy, reputation, feelings, and many other things at risk. Your presentation needs to inspire trust. Trust takes a long time to build. But there are shortcuts.

In 1984, psychologist Robert Cialdini released the book *Influence*. *Fortune* magazine lists *Influence* in their "75 Smartest Business Books." Warren Buffett and Charlie Munger said it is one of the most important books they've ever read! It's required reading for almost every psychology class and is one of the most cited psychology books in the world. It's also been meticulously studied and practiced by every ad agency and marketing company in the world.

In the original book, Cialdini outlines 6 principles of persuasion. In preparation for this book, he spent years undercover by riding shotgun and partnering up with every kind of salesperson and persuasion practitioner he could find to study what the very best innately knew and did to influence their customers. Door-to-door sales, used cars, real estate, life insurance, time-share sales, you name it.

Compiling the cumulative wisdom of his many years of academic studies, his personal research and experiences, he could boil down all significant influence methods into just these 6 principles. In 2021 he revised and updated the book, adding one more principle.

In this part of the book, I'll outline the general principles, give some examples of how they're used on us every day, and then provide some practical applications that you can use in your next presentation.

Before I do that, I'd like to briefly introduce you to his second book. It's called *Pre-suasion*. From the title, you might surmise that it's a combination of Pre (before) and Persuasion. And it's exactly that. It's about what you can do before your pitch, presentation, or speech to set things up in your favor. Some of these 7 principles can be used during and after your presentation. Some of them can be used beforehand.

I've created a pneumonic to help you remember the principles. It's an acronym. SCALES-U. Each letter represents one of the principles. I like to think of it as a metaphor. By adding one or more of these principles, you can tip the SCALES of persuasion to you (U) , or in your favor.

These principles are so strong that they occasionally work on Cialdini himself. I've spent years studying them and applying them; yet they still work on me from time to time. In his updated version of the book, he acknowledges this power and has added ways to deal with them when we are being targeted. I highly recommend the book.

Here they are. I'll go through each one and discuss the...

PRINCIPLE: A basic definition.

IN THE WILD: How you might observe it in your everyday life.

PRESENTATION APPLICATION: How you can adapt it to your next business presentation

# SCALES-U

## PRINCIPLE 1/ SCARCITY

"The way to love anything is to realize that it might be lost." - G.K. Chesterton

**PRINCIPLE**- People tend to value things they can't have. This means unique, rare, fleeting things, adding a sense of urgency.

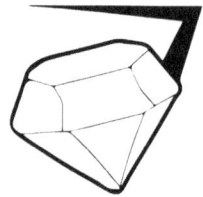

Another aspect of scarcity is appealing to the pain of losing something (also called loss aversion). Loss aversion states that the pain of loss hurts more than the joy of gaining something.

This principle also involves reactance. You can think of examples like forbidden love ala Romeo and Juliet or the forbidden fruit in Eden or the greener grass of distant pastures. People often want what they can't have.

**IN THE WILD**- This is probably one of the most commonly seen principles. When the Covid-19 pandemic started, there were rumors of a toilet paper shortage. This caused panic buying behavior in some people, and they stocked up in unreasonable ways. This is a survival instinct and is hard to fight.

When having a sale, most stores will have a sign advertising the event. It will usually be a red sign. Red is a color that evokes attention and urgency.

They will usually write about how much time is left before the sale ends, or make a plea to hurry. They will use phrases like "sale ends soon" or "while supplies last."

They may even limit how many items you can purchase, such as "only 2 per customer." This sounds like it's counterproductive for them since their goal is to sell more. In reality, studies have shown that sales actually go up by limiting the availability in these cases!

When booking a hotel room or airline ticket, you'll usually see a warning about how many are left, how many are left "at this price," when they expect to sell out, how many were recently sold, and often, how many other people are looking at it right now.

If you've never noticed this before, I guarantee you will see it everywhere now that you know.

### *PRESENTATION APPLICATION*

UNIQUE - What things are uncommon or unusual about your message? By distinguishing your proposal's uniqueness and showing how it differs from the others, you can get better attention, retention, and desirability. You can evoke creativity, exclusiveness, and elitism by showing its differences.

Ask yourself: How is your product, service, or company different? How is it unique? How does it stand apart from the crowd and thus merit attention? In sales, they call this the USP or Unique Selling Point. If everyone is pushing the same things with the same features, then the price is the only differentiator. In that case, it's a race to zero game with your competition. That is a race that you don't want to be in. There are no winners in a race to the bottom.

When designing your presentation, choose your main points in a way that differentiates your option from the rest. Show how no one else offers this or can bring the benefits that you offer. Think about how major brands do this. Often adding one unique feature can make you stand out and get attention.

For example, there is a lot of competition in my field of presentation coaches. To stand out, I've added a deep interest of mine, Behavioral Economics, to my business description. By adding this to my title, I've been able to attract the attention of many companies that certainly wouldn't have noticed me otherwise. One prominent advertising and marketing company noticed that I used Behavioral Science and Economics principles in my methodology and invited me to speak at their annual Behavioral Science event. This led to a lot of public exposure and to many lucrative training contracts with newly interested vendors. It was always there, but I had not highlighted that distinction before.

RARE- Things that are limited in supply. This can be due to many reasons. Lack of resources, logistical issues, legalities, availability, etc.

Point out any unique opportunities that exist, the possibility of never having the chance again, and the lengths others would go to in order to have the same opportunity.

Consider this: most of the diamond industry is run by one company. That company holds a vast storehouse of diamonds all around the world. They release it in small amounts to keep its image of being rare. The truth is, diamonds are nowhere near as rare as they let on. It's a superficial rarity created to keep the perceived value high, and thus the price even higher. Rarity adds a layer of perceived value.

Another way of appealing to the rareness of something is by highlighting the uniqueness of an offer or proposal. If someone feels that not everyone has the same opportunity as they are being offered right now, they may feel more compelled to take action. For example, where I live in Shanghai, the cost of a license plate for a car is around $15,000 USD. That's right, you heard correctly. It's been called the most expensive piece of sheet metal in the world.

But in addition to that obstacle, there's one more hurdle. The government strictly limits how many plates are released each month to reduce traffic congestion. You first need to apply for one, and then a limited amount of "winners" are picked in a lucky draw. I once had a client walk in excitedly – saying he finally won. "Oh, that's great!" I said. "What did you win?"

"A chance to buy a license plate!" he exclaimed. I tried to match his enthusiasm, but I couldn't help thinking that he was not as lucky as he thought. He felt lucky for the chance to buy something for $15,000 that I got in Brooklyn for around $25. The uniqueness of the lucky draw and the rarity of being chosen were high. So his perception of the value was also very high.

Try to show your audience why they are unique for having this opportunity. If there are ways in which they have an exclusive opportunity not given to everyone, make sure to highlight that and let them feel special.

Highlighting your audience's rare qualities is another way of using the power of scarcity. I'm not suggesting mere flattery here, but rather a deliberate emphasis on the positive attributes your audience possesses that will make them realize their privileged position. Are they the first you have offered this opportunity? Are they the only ones who will get the chance? Is it because of your relationship that you are offering this exclusive chance?

LOSS AVERSION- Many years ago Amos Tversky and Richard Thaler created Prospect Theory. They had noticed a strange phenomenon: there is greater pain in losing than joy in getting. The typical selling tactic outlines all the benefits and features a choice brings. While this can have a positive effect, sometimes people are content with what they have and aren't interested in more. In these situations, what often works better is to appeal to what they may lose instead. Realistically, people are more troubled by what they can lose if they don't choose your option.

There are many things that people can lose. There are obvious things such as money, time, or manpower.

But there are far more things that people value and will not part with if they can help it. Sometimes these things aren't tangible like money but are more abstract. Some examples are power, opportunity, competitive advantage, respect, authority, reputation, cost of replacement, status, authority, reputation, freedom, etc. Brain drain (the loss of critical people from a country or company) and FOMO (Fear Of Missing Out) are other forms of loss and can motivate people.

Try to point out what they will lose and paint a picture of what that would look like. The more they can imagine and actually feel the loss, the better.

For example, list off specific scenarios where their new reality would be disastrous. Recently I worked with a client who was trying to persuade his superiors to change a policy that was causing division in the company. Instead of focusing on the benefits of another policy, we used a loss aversion angle to show that they had already lost some talented staff and were poised to lose even more in the near future if things didn't change.

But we went one step further. We got in touch with HR and found out the cost of getting a headhunter to source replacements for those that left and those potentially leaving. We spoke to the training department to determine the actual costs of training inbound talents. We asked them to calculate the lost efficiency and decline in morale in the interim period. By doing the extra research and adding these factors, we increased the pain of losing staff in their minds.

In Behavioral Economics, there is something called the Endowment Effect. It is the observation that people put more value on things they currently have or own than on things they don't have. We see this in children early on as they learn to say "mine" very quickly.

For example, have you ever noticed that most people have difficulty lowering the price of something they are selling? Because it is theirs, they place a higher perceived value on the item. The same effect takes place when something they own is abstract. It can be a quality, a state of being, a privileged position, etc.

Remember that people ultimately want happiness , success, and freedom. Try to think of situations where losing something would impact their...

HAPPINESS- Negative effects on relationships, boredom, friction, reduced creativity, being forced to do more of the kind of work you hate.

SUCCESS- The potential to lose status, title, privilege, ability, reputation, salary, knowledge, or insights.

FREEDOM- Not being able to access/use/take advantage of/choose/participate in, etc.

You can also help them to reason on how a loss in status might affect them more significantly by illustrating it with a case study or example.

For example, I was working with a video game company that was about to launch a new game. These launches are well hyped, and there is a lot of buzz going on before each launch.

I was working with the developers, and they were almost ready to call it good except for some lingering bugs in the game.

The developers wanted to postpone the launch until the game was 100% bug-free. They just needed a little bit more time.

Headquarters didn't feel the same. They thought the game could be released and patches designed to fix the issues later. At the time, bugs were common, and it was relatively normal to fix issues after release.

The developers were not happy about this. They argued with HQ about how long and hard they had been working on this and how they wanted to be proud of the end result.

As usual, when you argue from the point of what you want, the other side rarely sees things the same way. So I met with them, and we looked over their situation. We focused not on what the developers wanted, but rather on what HQ might be concerned about.

We used the OREO structure to make our point.

O - OPINION: State your opinion.

R - REASON: Give a clear reason that they will agree with and is in their best interest.

E - EXAMPLE: Share an example that supports your reason.

O - OPINION: Restate your opinion for emphasis, summary, and as a call to action.

It went like this...

OPINION - The game shouldn't be released with bugs.

REASON - Releasing with bugs can ruin our reputation.

EXAMPLE - Company X released their game last year and were the joke of the industry for years.

OPINION: Therefore, I don't think we should release this game until it's bug-free.

Using the fear of losing their reputation and market share increased the persuasiveness of their argument.

URGENCY- A ticking clock raises cortisol – and therefore stress – quickly. Time is our eternal foe, and it waits for no one. When making a call to action, provide a timeline for your audience and show them why speed is of the essence. The thought of losing something will give people pause, but knowing that time is limited will drive action. Knowing that their competition has already done or is about to do the same will be a powerful driver toward taking an opportunity.

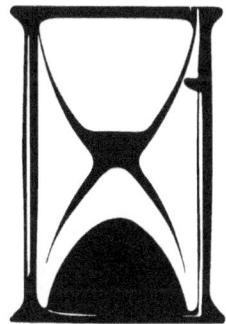

Always remember that you are often fighting against procrastination, hesitation, and deliberation. Doubt or uncertainty will cause them to hold back from making a decision. Time is usually against you in this case.

Is there limited or fleeting quantity or stock? Are others looking at it now as well, possibly their competition? Is it a limited-time offer? Is there a market shortage? Is there an impending price hike? Are relevant laws about to change? Have unknown hypotheticals been considered (such as Covid)? Is there market instability? You need to draw their attention to these factors and the consequences of disregarding them.

## PRINCIPLE 2/

## CONSISTENCY & COMMITMENT

*PRINCIPLE*- People want to be consistent in what they say and do and fulfill commitments they have made.

When presented with the similarities of what you are offering and the things they have already committed to (especially publicly), they are more likely to not deviate from their initial stance. In short, no one wants to be a hypocrite.

This is not about shaming someone. Rather it is merely reminding them of who they are and what they stand for. The real goal is to subtly highlight their stated stance on something and then hold up your idea next to it to show how it's the same or similar.

Commitment is about how people tend to feel obligated to follow through on things they've agreed to.

*IN THE WILD*- Reporters are quick to find flashbacks of politicians saying something long ago and then contrasting it with a recent statement or action. They do this because, once again, it's shameful to be a hypocrite.

People usually try to stay consistent with what was earlier stated when light is shown on previous statements, standards, or beliefs.

For example, my parents were approached by someone selling timeshares (a rental contract for vacation spots) at the beach. They were offered some free gifts for attending a brief pitch. My parents were ready to listen to a little sales pitch, say no, and walk away with their free gifts – or so they were hoping.

But the sales pitch didn't come. Early on, my parents said they were just curious and would probably not buy anything. So it seemed that the agent respected their determination.

The agent was friendly and not pushy at all. Instead, he asked them about their life and family. He shared some of his family pictures and they traded stories.

They talked for a while and actually relaxed a bit and enjoyed the conversation. After a while, he thanked them for coming and gave them their gifts.

As they were about to stand up and leave, the agent looked as if he had just remembered something. "Oh yeah, sorry, I forgot to show you the offer. My boss would kill me if I didn't at least show you the brochure!"

As he handed them the brochure, he began to restate everything they had told him. Each sentence started with "You said..." Such as: "You said that there was nothing you loved more in life than to have the whole family together on vacation." "You said that since your children are in different places around the world, it would be good to meet in a central location." He used their words to move them to action. Much to my chagrin, they bought a timeshare.

Now I'm not suggesting trying to talk people into things they don't want or need. These seven principles can be used for good as well as evil. All the principles in this book are intended to be used ethically. I'm just showing you the power of these principles.

For these principles to be used ethically, we must ensure that the audience benefits. Often we can help our audiences stay true to who they are, their company culture, or their branding by using a gentle reminder.

**PRESENTATION APPLICATION**- You can search the internet for things your audience have said in the past. Look for groups that they are affiliated with (and the principles they stand for), blogs, vlogs, emails, speeches, YouTube videos, mission statements, mottos, emails, quotes, interviews, banners, etc. You can remind them of these things to help them stay consistent.

If you've done your audience analysis well, you may have already come across different elements you can use with this principle. Once you find these, you can refer to them and show your agreement with them. You can talk about your respect for them, and your desire to help them to stay true to themselves, by acknowledging the similarities of your offering.

For example, I worked with an IT company a few years ago. The local team I was working with was in research and development. They wanted to change the software they were using to a new system. They made their pitch, but headquarters was against it and told them not to change it. Their reason was that it was too risky. They reached out to me to help.

After a few discussions to assess our options, we decided to try the pitch again. We researched the company's history, as well as its mission statement and company principles. Reading their history, I noticed that the CEO had started the business from his garage and later sold his house to finance the upstart. He was an all chips in kind of guy. It paid off. The company is now Fortune 500 listed and known for their innovations.

On examining their guiding principles, I came across one that stood out and aligned with our proposal: disruptive. We were able to use the CEO's backstory and the guiding principle of being disruptive to show that the claim of too risky didn't fit with the company's character or the CEO's philosophy of business.

We could drive the change they wanted because it was consistent with the company's DNA: Disruptive implies risk. This was a case of reminding them of who they were and where they came from.

Another way to utilize this principle is through a Commitment Ladder, or as some call it, a Yes Ladder. The principle has similarities to the old foot in the door technique.

You try to get your audience to agree to a small, general point early on and then slowly funnel that towards a bigger ask.

For example, "Here at the Acme Company, we have the motto 'People first!' So obviously, safety here is key, right? And we are really proud of our excellent safety record, correct? And wouldn't it just ruin everything if someone were to get seriously injured or even worse, die? So, of course, we are always looking for new ways to prevent tragedies before they happen, isn't that true?" Then you could make a pitch for some safety equipment, policy change, or whatever your call to action is.

Surprisingly, studies have shown that this technique can work even if the initial questions are not related to your main point. It just gets people into a more relatively compliant state.

Also, this can be a more drawn-out process covering several different pitches and presentations, each one slowly moving towards the ultimate goal. Instead of the big ask, you could ask for a trial period or just approval to investigate the option further.

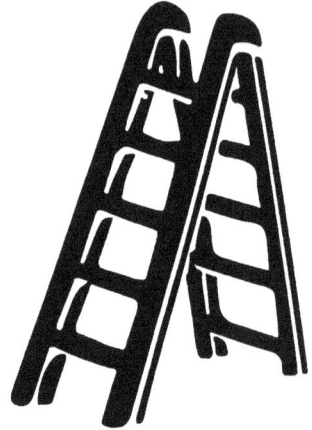

## PRINCIPLE 3/ AUTHORITY

*PRINCIPLE*- If someone appears to be an expert or authority on something, we are likely to believe and trust them.

You can present yourself as an authority or borrow from someone else's authority by quoting other experts, stating expert testimonials, etc.

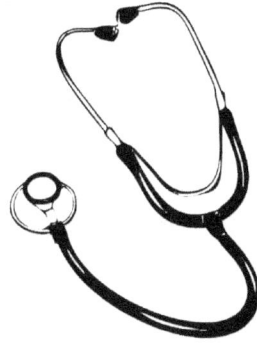

*IN THE WILD*- People will take medical advice from someone in a doctor's coat over someone in a T-shirt. If doctors display their medical degree on the wall behind them, people are more likely actually to follow their advice.

Celebrities endorse products all the time that they are not experts on. Often we will see commercials with famous performers wearing a doctor's coat with a stethoscope around their neck, saying, "I'm not a doctor, but I play one on TV...." And then pitch the product. We tend to believe their pitch because we trust those in lab coats. You will also hear the appeal to authority when a commercial says, "9 out of 10 doctors recommend..." Appeals to authority work.

*PRESENTATION APPLICATION*- For someone to view you as an expert or a professional, you need to display three main factors: credibility, character, and confidence.

CREDIBILITY- You need to show your audience that you are capable, competent, and/or certified. They need to see your skills, knowledge, experience, and education on the topic.

You can share testimonials of your success. I usually try to do this in story form. You can subtly drop in facts that exert your authority. Things such as your title/position, degrees and certifications, companies you've worked with, achievements, awards, etc. But a note of caution on that, because you may sound as if you're bragging, which can actually reverse the desired effect. It's better to be subtle and to not throw everything but the kitchen sink in there.

CHARACTER- Your audience needs to trust you as a person. People naturally protect themselves by judging the honesty, morals, and ethics of those who try to change them. The way you are perceived needs to be positive. Positive can mean different things to different people. Again, this doesn't mean just telling them that you are honest and transparent. Storytelling is a more subtle way of showing, not telling. As you're giving an example of something else, drop in small details highlighting your character.

You need to know your audience and speak their language. A simple faux pas can taint their vision of you so be careful with sensitive topics and avoid unnecessary controversies.

CONFIDENCE- They know that you are credible and of good character. But they need to feel it too. Everything they see and hear, from the tone of your voice to the posture and positioning of your body, will inform them, for better or for worse. How you walk and talk will be the lens through which they subconsciously judge the weight of your words.

We can show our authority in other ways too. The most important part is that the source of authority is higher than our audience. We can quote others who are known as experts. Awards from credible agencies , data, facts, and statistics from well-known sources such as business magazines, universities, or institutions are all good sources of authority.

I run regular training sessions for various multinationals. I usually show a slide briefly with all the logos of the companies I've worked for. They are all giant MNCs so just a quick look will inspire confidence in me. It starts off the training with a little bit of credibility.

I wouldn't do this in a normal presentation, though. The way I would do this is by telling a story. I usually find an opportunity to tell a story based on the topic we are discussing. I subtly mention which type of company the client was at, their position in the company, and the problem I helped them solve. Subconsciously they will pick up that I'm a credible and competent authority.

If we directly point to our authority or expert status, it can often come across as bragging and might not be believable. A great way to get around this is to elicit an introduction from someone else. It could be a colleague, a fellow presenter, or an event coordinator. By offering to help craft the introduction, we can write the things we can't say. If it comes from someone else, it has a lot more credibility, even though we wrote it, and even if the person introducing us has an equal amount to gain from the success of our presentation.

Authority is also something that we show in our body language and voice control. A wholehearted belief in our pitch is the foundation on which we should build our confidence. After that, knowing the audience and having a well-thought-out strategy will give us further courage.

Studying the fundamentals of public speaking is a must as well. But I have always noticed some speakers I've thought of as excellent do not always adhere to the commonly touted public speaking rulebook.

Confidence doesn't have clear rules, but we know it when we see it. So when practicing your presentations, video them and watch them back. Practicing in a mirror isn't the same because we naturally self-correct, and we can't observe the tone, timing, and timbre.

How we are dressed and groomed will affect how we are perceived. The general rule of thumb is to dress slightly better (more formal) than our audience. But it's good to realize many different psychological principles are frequently at play, even here.

For example, do you remember the Red Sneaker Effect? It's when someone wears something that makes them stand out, such as red sneakers. There is sometimes an increase in their perceived status. You might think of Mark Zuckerberg and his infamous hoodie. The one factor that makes this work is that it has to be deliberate. Someone whose clothing stands out because they have bad taste or no sense of style causes the opposite reaction, a loss of status. It has to be someone with the confidence to pull it off. There are always exceptions to the rules, so tread cautiously.

Overall, they have to feel that they can trust what we are saying. But even if they trust us, it doesn't always mean they like us. Let's talk about that next and see why it's so important.

# PRINCIPLE 4/ LIKING

*PRINCIPLE*- People tend to help and cooperate with people they like. Simple.

We like people who are similar to us, have mutual interests, or have some common ground.

We like people that help and support us.

We tend to like people we find physically attractive, or good-looking.

We also like people that make us feel good and make us feel safe. Safety is important when building trust, rapport, and connection.

*IN THE WILD*- We often see things like nepotism, where family members help each other out. We see

preferential treatment where the relationship is more important than the person's abilities.

*PRESENTATION APPLICATION*- There are things that you can do BEFORE you make your pitch. These would be things that help make a connection between you and your audience. How? Well, if it's someone we regularly see, then this is something that we can build up over time. This has to be a consistent and deliberate routine of showing interest, attention, and respect to them. If it's not someone you regularly see, can you make an effort to meet them right before the presentation?

Many presenters spend their last few minutes before a presentation psyching themselves up. Unless you have high pre-presentation anxiety, that time might be better spent building relationships with your audience. This will increase your likability and can often quell your nerves because now you actually know your audience, and it can take away a little bit of that fear of the unknown. It can be an essential component of your persuasion intervention.

This pre-presentation conversation part essentially comes down to our overall communication skills. If you can find out something personal about those in your audience, you will better be able to relate to them. Look for opportunities to get their feelings on the topic you will discuss. See if they have questions or comments about your topic. Remember or write down things they say that you may be able to reference in your presentation.

During the presentation, you can also increase likability. You can find ways to compliment your audience. The compliment needs to be sincere and genuine. It's always better if you say something about a work quality in a business context. For example, use adjectives such as creative, innovative, resourceful, etc., or comment on their communication skills, work ethic, stress management, composure, organization skills, etc.

The interesting thing about compliments is that when we associate a quality with a person, we naturally start to like them. This is good because people can often tell if it's genuine or not.

Another bonus is that when you associate someone with a positive quality, and you verbalize that to them, they will often associate that same quality with you.

For example, if I call you trustworthy, you will also tend to believe that I am also somewhat trustworthy. Otherwise, you can't accept my opinion/compliment. And we all secretly love and want to believe compliments! These need to be natural and sincere. Try to think of things people work hard at and are proud of. Sure, you can say "nice glasses," but if you compliment a trait that shows their character, it will be much more impactful.

Also, when you find out things that people like, you can incorporate that into your presentation. This will create a comfortable and familiar environment for them. If you like the same thing, that's even better. But just speaking their language by talking about things they like and have an interest in will affect how your message lands.

Recently I had a client who had trouble communicating with his director. When I asked about what the director was interested in, he immediately said golfing. "Every presentation he makes has a golf reference, illustration, or picture!" he said. So I encouraged him to slightly mirror this behavior. He started to incorporate similar concepts and then even check with the boss to see if his golfing illustrations were correct. Often they weren't but the boss talked his ear off explaining the golf concepts. Quickly the dynamic between them improved, and it spilled over into their professional relationship. Learn the language of other people's hearts!

Sharing stories and vulnerabilities can also lend to likability. When we tell not just our success stories but also our failure stories, trust and likability will increase. Don't only tell failure stories, but don't be afraid to pepper them in once in a while.

HUMOR- "In those whom I like, I can find no common denominator; In those whom I love I can: They all make me laugh." – W.H. Auden

Humor is like a Swiss army knife. If used correctly, it can set the tone of a relationship. It can be used to change the subject, divert focus, lower stress, defuse tense situations, increase memory, boost bonding, disarm your audience, lower defenses, make a hard point indirectly or without appearing critical, add life to a boring topic, engage and hold attention, and finally, increase your likability.

It can make you look more relatable, caring, likable, and trustworthy.

But if used incorrectly, it can fall on deaf ears, hurt feelings, and lose trust. It can make you look more careless, indifferent, and insensitive. It can be a double-edged sword.

The most-watched TED Talk is Ken Robinson's talk on creativity. It has over 21 million views. He has a dry wit, but in his first five minutes, he made people laugh at a rate of 2 laughs per minute (LPM)! For reference, the movie *Airplane!* was 3LPM, *The Hangover* was 2.4LPM, *Superbad* was 1.9LPM, *Borat* was 1.7 LPM, and *Anchorman* was about 1.6 LPM.

But you may be saying, "I'm not giving TED Talks. I'm trying to run a serious business. They won't respect me, and they'll think I'm a joke."

Well, an important distinction is what type of humor you're employing and what tone it's given in. For example, sarcasm is great for comedians and movie performers but can backfire and damage a relationship if not wielded correctly.

Self-deprecating humor on the other hand very rarely offends, if ever. Self-deprecating humor is when you point out eccentricities, weaknesses, and quirks in your own behavior.

One of the key factors in Emotional Intelligence (EQ) is self-awareness. Self-awareness is about knowing your own emotions, strengths, and weaknesses. Self-deprecating humor is focused on this. A leader who can be comfortable, confident, and candid will increase trust through their transparency.

Trust is the foundation of all relationships; business is no exception. Being self-aware and open to sharing your observations is a sign of confidence. Insecure people are not able to share their weaknesses.

Eminem's famous rap battle in the movie *8 Mile* comes to mind. In a tense scene, where the battle is heating up, Eminem takes his turn. Instead of focusing on his rival's weaknesses, he first points out his own weaknesses. By making fun of himself first, he comes across as self-aware and yet calm, cool, and confident. The audience erupts in cheering. He wins the battle by winning the crowd over.

Of course, you would want to do this in moderation. If you were constantly talking about your weaknesses, you would surely come across as neurotic.

Also, you need to be cautious about core skills, character, or anything that would directly undermine your audience's perception of your leadership. If done in excess or inauthentically, it can come across as insincere, or even be perceived as fishing for compliments. My advice is always to test it out around the office first and see what lands and what doesn't before you take it to the stage in your next presentation.

Other types of humor can be very effective but often come with caveats. Sarcasm has been shown to increase the audience's perception of the speaker's intelligence and confidence. But it's important that your audience feels psychologically safe and secure. If that line is crossed, trust will diminish, and a willingness to collaborate will disappear.

Don't isolate, alienate, or discriminate. Inside jokes increase group cohesion and invoke the unity principle for those that get it, while at the same time alienating and isolating those who don't.

Comments aimed at a race, culture, age, gender, or other socially sensitive topics need to be weeded out. Profanity, off-color comments, or other insensitive remarks will often have mixed reactions, so consider your entire audience.

Be cautious with aggressive humor – making fun of others – as the audience usually perceives it negatively. If this is something that you have a hard time with, and you are not good at reading the room or getting a laugh, tread carefully with this one. You can try a little at a time and see what works in different situations.

Also, studies have shown that in different cultures, humor in presentations is perceived differently for men and women, so please take that into consideration.

But most importantly, we need to take a look at the persuasive power of humor.

"If I can get you to laugh with me, you like me better, which makes you more open to my ideas. And if I can persuade you to laugh at the particular point I make, by laughing at it, you acknowledge its truth." – John Cleese (comedian of Monty Python fame)

Humor puts people in a relaxed, safe, and happy frame of mind. It lowers defenses and opens up minds. This is precisely the state you want if you want to win hearts and minds.

So as you prepare your next presentation, think about ways you can positively incorporate a little humor, if appropriate. A funny quote, picture, or anecdote can lighten up an otherwise mundane presentation.

An interesting observation or an ironic analogy can logically make a point and get your audience to reason on your point with a relaxed, calm mind.

And adding physical comedy to your narratives can engage your audience as you act out scenarios and dialogues with your body language and vocal variety.

# PRINCIPLE 5/ EXCHANGE/RECIPROCITY

***PRINCIPLE*** - Reciprocity is the natural obligation we feel to repay a favor or kindness shown. This is universal; every culture appreciates gifts and desires to repay anyone who has helped them or shown a cooperative spirit. It's often re-ferred to as "give to get."

***IN THE WILD*** - It's probably one of humans' most natural and beautiful in-stincts to want to reciprocate kindness and goodness. If someone gives us a gift or shares, we automatically feel obligated to repay, give back, or share however possible.

I see this used everywhere in marketing and advertising. Last time I visited my parents, I noticed a stack of calendars on one of the chairs. My mom sighed and said that many charities had sent her a calendar. This would be accompanied by a request for a donation. This "free gift" ploy is powerful.

"So, did you donate?" I asked.

"Well, yeah, they had to pay for the printing, so that was the least I could do."

I asked how much she gave on average, and let's just say it was probably about a 1,000% ROI for the calendars.

In China, there is a principle called Guanxi. It is the principle of repaying a favor. Interestingly, the favor given first is often repaid later at a higher return.

Reciprocity builds relationships and trust.

***PRESENTATION APPLICATION***- Share value. Provide something your audience can take away and make their life better.

Offering something for free, such as coaching, advice, a trial period of service, or whatever engages the principle of reciprocity.

Also, giving doesn't have to be a physical gift. In our current business climate, giving physical gifts is often equated with bribery. But there are a host of things that can be considered gifts that are intangible yet valuable.

Honestly, one of the most valuable things we can give someone these days is our time and attention. Any chance you have to show your clients or audience that you are willing to share your time and attention is an opportunity to evoke the power of reciprocity. Ask questions, show a genuine interest, respond promptly, and ease the friction in their lives, and they will reciprocate in kind.

In my training business, I've found that my desire to reduce my clients' friction in their daily business has vastly improved my relationships with them.

If I point out how I'm doing something that will lessen their workload or stress, they always reward me with loyalty and respect. Adding value by helping people to do their job better, more efficiently, receive recognition, or have more impact is a gift often greater than money itself.

In presentations, you can give a gift to your audience by sharing valuable insights, tips and tricks, understandings, or information they didn't already possess.

This works internally in a company by sharing your day-to-day realizations and insights with upper management or externally by giving your clients the latest scoop on what's happening from your vantage point. This works great when you have nothing to gain from this information except relationship building and trust.

You can build trust and rapport simply by remembering things about a person. I often start my training workshops by telling about some of my personal hobbies and passions and then asking the participants what they love to do for fun. This is a simple question. Yet when I work that into my presentations later with them, they are often amazed and flattered that I remembered their particular passions. This is the same with personal facts about them. Where are they from? What are their family circumstances? What are their passions?

This might not seem to be related to actual presentations, but it's more of the long game, if you will. With liking we spoke of building up rapport with someone. Similarly, with reciprocity, we know that our relationship before the actual presentation is equal to or sometimes way more important than our actual presentation. When we think of the principle of priming, we know that what happens right before our messaging is majorly important. So all we do in our everyday life builds rapport with our audience. If we are personally connected with our audience on social media, simple acts, such as liking things they would be proud of, can be extremely powerful. Look for ways to show your audience that you care about the same things that they do.

**Learnings from the Leather Apron Club**

Unlike the more straightforward effect of reciprocity, where you give to get, the Ben Franklin Effect involves a gift in a different way. It's different from simple reciprocity in the initiation of the effect. Instead of giving something to someone else to build a relationship, you ask them to give something to you. Yes, you heard correctly. Feel free to read that again.

Let me tell you how it worked with Benjamin Franklin. He's known for many things, including being a polymath. He was a politician, a publisher, a scientist, and a diplomat. It's this diplomatic edge he had that makes the Benjamin Franklin Effect work.

He was born one of 17 children to a low-income family. His father was a soap and candle maker. This was the lowliest of artisan crafts at the time. But he was a curious child. He worked hard and learned about everything he could.

In 1727 Benjamin Franklin started a club for acquaintances to gather on Friday nights and share stories, ideas, and observations. They spoke of science, poetry, morals and ethics, philosophy, and business.

Benjamin was the leader and called it the Junto Club, based on the Spanish word for "assembly." He also called it the Leather Apron Club. He was a social man and had an intense drive to learn and improve.

Soon this club started discussing books. Books were hard to come by in those days. As they read the more well-known books, they needed to get their hands on more. Benjamin decided to start America's first subscription library. This way, he could get access to all the books he wanted, help the Junto, and make some profit.

As his political career moved on, he found that he would make a few enemies once in a while, just due to differences in politics. One such man was a political rival. This man wouldn't even speak to Benjamin in public. The man was rich and powerful and Benjamin wanted to have this man as an ally, not an enemy. But how?

Benjamin studied this man well and knew what he cared about. He hatched a plan.

Benjamin narrates the account in his autobiography. "I did not aim at gaining his favor by paying any servile respect to him, but after some time took this other method. Having heard he had in his library a certain very scarce and curious book, I wrote a note to him expressing my desire of perusing that book and requesting he would do me the favor of lending it to me for a few days. He sent it immediately, and I returned it in about a week with another note expressing strongly my sense of the favor.

"When we next met in the House, he spoke to me (which he had never done before), and with great civility; and he ever after manifested a readiness to serve me on all occasions, so that we became great friends, and our friendship continued to his death."

Benjamin Franklin's conclusion: "He that has once done you a kindness will be more ready to do you another, than he whom you yourself have obliged."

In other words, people that do you a favor tend to like you.

Researchers have studied this and found it to be true. The exact reason is still not 100%, but there are theories. Some feel it's a result of cognitive dissonance. This is the uncomfortable feeling you have when your beliefs and reality conflict. So, in this case, "Why would I do nice things for someone I hate? I must like them."

Other researchers have hypothesized that it's due to the Self-perception Effect. This is where we look to our actions to inform our feelings about things. It's like when you start to ask yourself if you're falling for someone: "I do spend a lot of time talking to her..." "I don't like it when I see other guys talk to her... I must like her!"

But also notice that Benjamin Franklin studied his subject and knew the man was proud of his rare book collection. He was flattered that someone had noticed. So there is a little bit of taking the first step to notice and verify as valuable something that someone else has, does, or is.

OK, so how can this be used in presentations? How can you get someone to do you a favor as you're presenting? Well, this is another case of pre-presentation rapport building.

If you have someone you regularly present to, and they give you a hard time or disagree with you often, changing your arguments will most likely bring more of the same.

One of my clients had someone in her office that always gave her a hard time and loved to shoot down her ideas. He would always make sarcastic remarks about her presentations. So I asked her if she would be willing to go to him and ask him for help. She resisted at first but reluctantly she said that she would try.

"I have a presentation this week and I just wanted to run something by you to get your feedback. Would you mind?" The man was flattered that she asked him for advice and deemed his feedback as valuable. He obliged, listened, and gave her feedback. The result?

Not only did he not give her a hard time but he actually defended her a bit when someone else started to try to poke holes in her presentation.

Why? The Benjamin Franklin Effect and the fact that now he was slightly invested as her mentor of sorts. Psychology works.

## PRINCIPLE 6/ SOCIAL PROOF

*PRINCIPLE*- We tend to follow the things that people who are like us do, like, or feel.

Whereas with the authority principle we tend to look toward people who are more experienced, wiser, and skilled, with social proof, we look to our peers.

*IN THE WILD*- Think of herd mentality, native advertising, and product placement. You can also think of this as a word-of-mouth type effect. It can also be seen negatively as groupthink, or bandwagoning, where individuals follow the group blindly.

A more common observation is when we look to go to a hotel or vacation spot. The hotel says that it is beautiful and clean, and the staff is polite. It has won a few awards, speaking to the principle of authority. But we often go down to the comment section and look at what people like us, the users, are saying.

The reason for this can be conformity issues but often it's a trust in numbers thing. Our brain is always looking for shortcuts to make a good decision. It's betting all the time on what is most likely the best choice.

*PRESENTATION APPLICATION*- So when using this principle, you need to reference someone who is a peer of your audience. If you are speaking to a CEO, a similar CEO would be a good reference point. If you are talking to a colleague, you can reference what you and other similar colleagues are doing.

If you are selling a product, service, or concept, look for testimonials of other people who are similar to your audience. If we say these things about ourselves, it holds no weight.

When making a statement, back it up with a story, example, or case study that proves your exact point. Try to find an example where the people involved are similar to your audience.

Also, sometimes using their competition as an example can fuel both the principles of social proof and scarcity as they naturally will want to stay competitive.

Look for opportunities to share your social proof as a story. Instead of just saying that 80% of our colleagues use this – tell of a situation where you discovered that almost everyone in the office was using something. Then you can hit the 80% statistic for reinforcement.

Just beware of this effect because it can also work against you. When people know that many others are doing something, it gives them a pass to do it. This is called negative social effect.

For example, I could say that most people in this office come in late, but please come on time. I could give you many reasons, such as how it shows respect for the company, others, and clients. No matter what moral, ethical, or scientific reasons I give, the audience already knows that most people do it, so it's "normal." It will be an uphill battle for you.

So whenever you say that many or most people are doing something, please make sure it's the thing that you actually want them to do.

# PRINCIPLE 7/ UNITY

***PRINCIPLE*-** We tend to go along with those with whom we share an identity: people of our tribe. So this is not necessarily people who are "like us." It's people who "are us."

***IN THE WILD*-** Think of it like family. You may have very little in common with your family regarding tastes and preferences, but you have an inalienable affinity with them and thus would do anything for them.

Think of it as your in-group; your tribe. Think of how kids in school flock together due to a liking for one kind of music or fashion. Think of how people get competitive and territorial over brands, such as Apple vs. Microsoft. Think of sports fanatics who live, die, and would kill for their team.

Be cautious; this principle can unite people, but it can divide them just as easily. Think of patriotism, nationalism, or even racism.

***PRESENTATION APPLICATION*-** Building a feeling of family, community, or identity is bonding and very powerful. Mostly this will be done over time before the presentation if you're familiar with your audience.

If you're unfamiliar with them, try to meet them beforehand and find common ground. When you find it, let them see and share your excitement about that common ground so they view it as a bonding moment. Ask them lots of questions and get them to express why they are so passionate about it and what aspects appeal to them most. This will form a positive memory connection with you and the topic.

In other presentations, you can look for ways to point out a common, uniting aspect that the whole room shares. Think of common terms that people use to identify themselves.

What traits or characteristics do they all share?
Is everyone working for the same company?
Is everyone from the same place?
Does everyone share a trade or passion? Hackers, coders, engineers, creatives, techies, etc.

Within companies, you can highlight company culture and use the company's name to in-group everyone. You can also cite common core beliefs, mottos, or mission statements. For example, "At Apple, we all 'Think different.'"

Sometimes, depending on the size of the group and the topic, and other factors, you can use social ties like religious, political, or geographical commonalities to bond over. Obviously, you would need to use caution and avoid this becoming a divisive rather than uniting principle.

Oxytocin is known as the "love drug" because it's a neurotransmitter equated with bonding and unity. It's the chemical released when a mother first sees her child, when a man falls in love, and when we have sympathy for someone. It encourages a close bond, generosity, and even charity towards the other party.

But what you may rarely hear about is the fact that oxytocin only has that effect towards your in-group. It can cause an irrational hatred for a rival out-group. Think of rival gangs, opposing sports teams, or warring countries.

So when you evoke oxytocin, please think about the ripple effects and how it can affect different groups in your audience. If people are not definitely identified, they will feel ostracized and rejected.

And last, don't forget to use stories to exemplify your points. Stories are a great way to engage your audiences and a good story can be remembered forever.

Takeaways

Principles Of Persuasion – SCALES-U

- SCARCITY: People put value on things that are rare, unique, urgent, or appeal to loss aversion. People value freedom, happiness, and success. Show them how those things might be in jeopardy if they fail to change.

- COMMITMENT & CONSISTENCY: People want to stay consistent with things they have stated they believe in or their promises for the future.

- AUTHORITY: People tend to believe the words and opinions of experts and authorities. Credibility, character, and confidence are needed to be perceived as an authority.

- LIKING: People tend to help, collaborate, and cooperate with people they like. We like people that are similar to us, help us, or complement us. We also tend to trust and like people that make us laugh.

- EXCHANGE / RECIPROCITY: People tend to feel obligated to others who give to them first. Also, the Benjamin Franklin Effect can be used to build rapport.

- SOCIAL PROOF: People tend to follow other people who are in a similar situation, level, or position as them.

- UNITY: People tend to follow those who are of the same tribe or family as themselves

# BRIDGES: WHAT'S THE STORY MORNING GLORY?

.

"...in many ways the story of bridge building is the story of civilization. By it we can readily measure an important part of a people's progress."

**Franklin D. Roosevelt**

O NE DOESN'T JUST WAKE up with experience and wisdom. It takes time. And so it was also with John Roebling, the chief engineer of the Brooklyn Bridge. He was born on June 12, 1806, in Prussia. He graduated with a degree from the Royal Polytechnic School in Berlin. His thesis was on suspension bridges, an obsession he would continue to dwell on throughout his whole life.

He was very fond of his philosophy professor, Frederick Hegel. Hegel was a highly esteemed and world-famous professor of logic. John was the professor's favorite student, and the two were quite close.

John was determined to build bridges as an engineer. Hegel told him that he could never do that in Germany due to the bureaucracy. He told John that the logical thing was to learn English and move to America. And so he did. In 1831 John Roebling sailed to America.

His first job was not building bridges but working for a canal company. Here he observed the barges getting pulled up the canal with large, heavy hemp ropes. These ropes often failed under extreme loads and dirty conditions. On one such occasion, he shockingly watched as two men were instantly killed by a rope that suddenly snapped.

This got him thinking – "there has to be a better way!" He found the specifications to make a twisted wire rope in a German journal. He devised a machine and methodology to make this himself, and soon he was building small structures held up by his twisted wire rope.

In 1848 he opened his own wire company in Trenton, New Jersey. There is still a statue there in his honor. In 1851 he began to build a bridge at Niagara Falls. A few years into the building in 1854, he got word that another bridge over the Ohio River had just collapsed. Subsequently, he added some extra features to his bridge to fortify and reinforce key areas. But public sentiment continued to grow weary of these bridges. These collapses were happening more often in one place after another.

After a few years of engineering and overseeing the construction of a few more suspension bridges successfully, John Roebling had built quite a good reputation for himself. By the time the New York Bridge Company started raising money for a bridge in 1867, he was the obvious choice to build it.

But this bridge would be different. The span was immense. Longer than had ever been built. And that would make the towers carrying the cables even taller than any before. The Brooklyn Bridge was to be the tallest structure in the country at the time. Not only was the river an obstacle for John Roebling, but he had to overcome the people's doubt, apprehension, and trepidations. This would take a clear strategy and a confident pitch.

And this is what he set out to do. He designed a strategy to conquer the river's unique dimensions with mathematical calculations. He designed the bridge to withstand 6X the forces it needed to withstand. And he built the bridge with grandiose architecture meant to instill a feeling of awe and reverence in anyone who would cast their gaze upon it. With all those considerations in mind and a clear strategy to conquer them, he moved ahead with planning the project.

But the people were still worried and weary.

# TEN-STORY LOVE SONG

You don't really know someone until you know their story.

In the beginning of this book I used the *in media res* technique of starting the story in the middle of the action. People were dying, there was a mystery illness afoot, and the bridge was already started. This technique stirs up interest and intrigue. Who was this person? How did they die? What happened next? What can I learn from this?

John Roebling likely meant nothing to you before, and he immediately died in the book. Yet by learning just a little about his background, he becomes someone to you.

I wanted to highlight the story of Emily because it was so powerful and was more related to my theme. Yet, John Roebling's story is also very powerful in its own right, as you can see above. None of us likely has led such a turbulent and eventful life, yet his story didn't illuminate my point so I chose to use it later on, here.

Storytelling is one of the most powerful and natural methods of communicating. As the expert storyteller and Behavioral Science author Rory Sutherland of Ogilvy UK recently said, "Stories are like PDFs." By that he meant that they are a universally accepted and understood format for sharing information; they work for everybody.

# You don't really **know someone** until you know their **story**

Yet storytelling, to many, is often mysterious, mystical, and misunderstood. We all know what a story is but may have difficulty actually defining it. Even if you ask 10 storytelling experts (and I have), you will get 10 different definitions. Some fundamentals, though, are usually agreed upon.

A story, in its simplest form, is a telling of connected events. What makes a good story, though, is a whole other story. If we simply tell connected events that happened in chronological order, we are just reciting history. Although history has the word "story" in it, it's often a terrible form of storytelling. Why? Simply telling what occurred in the past without contextual background, relevant details, and takeaways for the listener is often boring, confusing, and meaningless.

I often have clients that include a "history of the company" slide in their presentations. It's often  the first one I ask them to take out. It's not that you can't have one, but if it doesn't tell the audience a story, it's often useless, and thus ignored by the audience. It's the same with business reports. You can report what happened by telling what occurred chronologically on a timeline – but this is not an engaging story. This is mere history.

So what, then, makes for a *good* story?

A good story needs more than just a list of factual events in the proper sequence.  I'll tell you what makes a good story in a minute, and don't worry, I'll even give you a simple structure to help you organize and sequence your stories. But first, let's spend a few minutes on the unique effects storytelling can have on your audiences.

Since there are many books on storytelling in general, I'll focus here on the Behavioral Science and psychological aspects of storytelling.

Many psychological and physiological changes occur when the brain encounters information told in narrative form.

### *PHYSIOLOGICAL*

I spoke earlier about the role that emotions play in decision making. I also spoke about how you need to specify what you want your audience to think, feel, or do. So when choosing and crafting your story, it's good to determine which emotion you would like to elicit. The story content, the way we tell it, and our audience's perception will dictate how they react.

Jeremy Connell-Waite is the Global Communication designer at IBM. He is a master storyteller and communicator. He is passionate about presentations that change the world and he has done just that with many of his business presentations as well as his activism. He recently had an epiphany about how to utilize emotions as a catalyst for change.

In an online interview he said, "There are hundreds of emotions but only 8 primary emotions. There are 5 survival emotions and 2 attachment emotions. Survival emotions are fear, anger, disgust, shame, and sadness."

He pointed out that "the vast majority of executives are overwhelmed and fearful. Scared of losing their jobs, scared of losing out to automation, to performance management. We have an average of 70,000 thoughts a day on average, 90% are the same as yesterday, and about 80% are negative. So most of us are operating with a negative mindset. These are the people we are trying to help. But we need to bring in positive emotions."

He then explained how the positive emotions work. "The 2 attachment emotions are love (and trust), and joy (and excitement). Love and trust are connected to oxytocin. Joy and excitement are connected to dopamine. Usually we are coming from a positive space and the people that we're trying to influence...are negative mindset. How do you flip from one to the other? The 8th emotion is surprise. It is a potentiator."

So , when you craft your stories, be very aware of areas where you can utilize surprise as a catalyst to change. Look for twists, revelations, and epiphanies that you can share to jostle your audience out of their comfort zones and into a state ready for change.

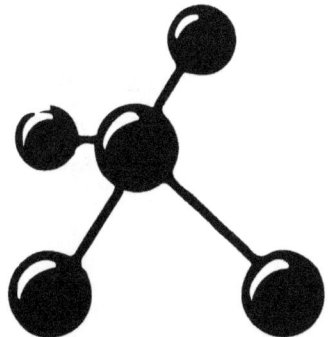

The brain releases different chemicals
to help us to make decisions and im-
print important events and details in our memories. When you
have vivid experiences, your brain chemically marks these memories. Your brain then mechanically reinforces these memories
by strengthening the synaptic connections. Here are some of the
more common chemicals your brain uses and their effect on you.

DOPAMINE- The reward and pleasure chemical. It raises focus
and motivates you to stay engaged and pay attention. It creates
needs and wants. Cliffhangers, thrillers, suspense, and mysteries
keep you in the zone. When dopamine is present, things are more
memorable. If you use interest, intrigue, suspense, and surprise,
dopamine levels will stay high.

Pace your story slowly and give subtle clues as you go, telling the
audience only the information you knew each step of the way. Try
holding back key pieces of information in the beginning to keep
them guessing, and feel free to throw in details that can serve to
misdirect their attention. This will keep them engaged and alert.

OXYTOCIN- Often called the "love drug" or "cuddle chemical." It
gives you a warm and fuzzy feeling. It's released during times of
emotional connection. It builds trust, empathy, sympathy, bonding, and evokes positive memories. It helps you connect with your
audience. And most importantly, it motivates your audience to not
just FEEL something – but DO something.

Sharing personal stories, displaying vulnerabilities, and sharing
weaknesses will build trust and make you more relatable. It will
also make them feel better about themselves. We all like people
that make us feel better about ourselves. Failure stories where we
learn a valuable lesson can also trigger oxytocin.

SEROTONIN- A neurotransmitter that modulates mood, cognition, reward, learning, and memory. It is known to be a mood booster and can produce a euphoric effect. Stories that are comforting, give hope, encourage, and allay fears are serotonin boosters.

ENDORPHINS- The feel-good drug, known for being related to the runner's high. Happiness, positivity, and optimism are some of the effects of endorphins. Physically you will tend to feel less pain when

endorphins are flowing. Imagine being depressed, and you stub your toe on a chair. It hurts sooo much! Now imagine winning 10 million dollars, and as you jump in celebration, you stub your toe on that same chair. You probably wouldn't even feel it.

Inspirational stories that make your audience feel alive will boost endorphins. Also, funny stories that make your audience crack up will have the same effect. Stories that focus on your audience's past, present, or potential success are sure to spike endorphins too.

CORTISOL- The stress hormone, usually released during stressful or anxious times. It can make someone physically warm up and start to sweat. It will also increase attention and trigger memories. You want to be careful with this because it is a negative emotion. Sometimes your audience needs to feel motivated to action. If they are apathetic or unconcerned and we know that it's in their best interest to change, we can stir up a little cortisol to light a fire under them.

Pain points are what salespeople call areas that cause the customer trouble, worry, or fear. A good story can show not just the benefits of our ideas but also the negative consequences of NOT adopting our proposals.

ADRENALINE- A hormone that regulates visceral functions like breathing and heartbeats. It's usually released in times of fight, flight, or freeze mode. It can make someone physically shake, stutter, or become paralyzed.

Similar to cortisol, we need to be careful with this one. A story that puts your audience in the driver's seat or shotgun to the action will raise their attention and drive focus. The effects can last a bit so remember to slowly transition to the next emotional state to give it time to wear off.

## *PSYCHOLOGICAL*

Some accompanying psychological effects can come into play as far as storytelling is concerned.

### IDENTIFIABLE VICTIM EFFECT

"If only one man dies of hunger, that is a tragedy. If millions die, that's only statistics." This quote is often attributed to Joseph Stalin and sums up a quintessential truth – we react to individual stories, not statistics.

Charities have long figured out that referencing large numbers of the sick and the dead doesn't really sink in or affect people as much as a photograph, an actual name, and an accompanying story of just one of those that are suffering.

So when crafting your stories, use real case studies and examples. Describe the characters vividly and in detail. People will picture them in their heads and thus be better able to relate to them. Find common ground between the hero in your story and your audience. Better yet, make your audience the story's hero and paint a picture of how your product, service, or idea will help them avoid problems and change their life for the better!

Also, try using personification when speaking about your company, product, or service. Give them human characteristics and a personality. If the audience can relate in some way, they are more likely to actually care. If they care, they are more likely to take action.

When you speak about your colleagues and teams, use storytelling elements by describing who they are, what they want, and how they solve issues to make your client's life and business better.

**IKEA EFFECT**- The tendency to highly value things you took part in creating, building, or discovering yourself.

Researchers observed this effect when they noticed that people who put their IKEA furniture together (an often frustrating task, especially for people like me who absolutely refuse to read the directions) place a higher value on it than on the same piece of furniture preassembled. They also tend to disregard any flaws in the outcome and regard them as character.

Do you remember I mentioned the Illusion of Control earlier and added this quote? "People don't resist change, they resist being changed." – Peter Senge. Yes, this is the foundational principle behind the IKEA effect.

When we are pushy or come across as salesy, people register that, reactance kicks in, and they dig their heels in to resist. But if you can subtly plant an idea in their head and get them to water and nurture it, they will take ownership of it to fruition. Or to continue the IKEA illustration, they will put it together in their minds and value it as if it were their own idea.

Storytelling is a fantastic way to accomplish this. By telling a story about someone else or another company, it allows them to make the inferences, see the similarities, and hopefully draw the correct conclusion. They will be more likely to follow through on the decision because it came from them.

So give them all the pieces, give them a picture of what success looks like, gently guide them to assemble it correctly, and sit back and watch them take pride in the work of their hands.

**ZEIGARNIK EFFECT-** The tendency for interrupted tasks to be remembered more than completed tasks.

In 1927, Russian psychologist Bluma Zeigarnik wrote about a curious phenomenon. She noticed that waiters could remember, with striking accuracy, all of an individual customer's orders throughout many stages of the meal. But that brilliant recall ended abruptly after the bill was paid. After that, she found that the waiters had difficulty recalling the same details they knew just minutes before. What was happening?

It seems that the brain subconsciously keeps working on unfinished tasks until they are finished. After that, it's a data dump unless those memories are chemically marked for long-term storage. How can you apply this to storytelling?

In most business presentations, I observe a data dump right from the get-go. A PowerPoint slide with all the facts, stats, graphs, and charts crammed together.

The audience can read faster than the presenter can speak. So they skim the content looking for useful, relevant (to them), or interesting information. Then they come up with a conclusion of their own on what the data is saying, dump all the irrelevant information, and then (maybe) tune back to the presenter, who is only halfway through reading out all the text. Not only boring but ineffective.

The audience came up with their own conclusion before the presenter could guide them. They've already finished the task themselves, and they've most likely dumped the data because no chemical markers were telling their brain to keep it in long-term memory.

Utilizing the Zeigarnik Effect, you could tell the information like a story. You can go through the stages one by one. You can show some missteps and dead ends, misdirecting them at times, adding details slowly, and holding back a few key details until the end. Your audience should be mouthing the words "And then what happened?" If you manage to keep intrigue and suspense high, attention and engagement will follow.

It's much like telling a joke. If you give all the information away right in the beginning, the audience might figure it out on their own, ruining the punchline. It's the same with expressing your ideas. Your audiences will stay engaged as long as they don't know the ending. The brain naturally wants to solve puzzles and decode riddles. And while it's doing that, it will focus its attention on that task and mark that information as something to keep long-term. When we hear a story, our brains go into problem solving mode. This not only keeps us engaged, it puts us in a judgment and decision making frame of mind. This is perfect for persuasion.

If you manage to keep **intrigue and suspense** high **attention and engagement** will follow

## The SHORT Story formula

So now that you know some of the amazing effects stories can produce and why you should tell them, let's talk about how to get started in strategic storytelling.

First, let's get back to the point of what makes for a good story.

Boy meets girl and they fall in love. They date and then get married. And they eventually have 3 beautiful children and happily grow old together. This is not much of an interesting story.

Boy meets girl, they fall in love, _but_ an unexpected event like war separates them, or society doesn't approve of their relationship, or the parents forbid them to see each other – like Romeo and Juliet – this makes for an engaging storytelling.

It's the _but_ part that makes it interesting and intriguing. It introduces conflict. The creators of the television series _South Park_ also realized this fact. They use a guiding principle that they refer to as the "rule of replacing _ands_ with _buts_ and _therefores_."

"Whenever you can exchange your _ands_ with _buts_ or _therefore_, it makes for better writing." – Trey Parker

Instead of just telling linked events in chronological order...
...and then this happened
...and then this happened
...and then this happened
...they replace the word _and_ with _but_ and then _therefore._

This is commonly known as the ABT storytelling system, developed by Dr. Randy Olsen and introduced in his book _Houston, We Have a Narrative: Why Science Needs a Story,_ published in 2015.

In it he explains that *and* sets up the situation, *but* introduces the conflict, and *therefore* presents a resolution. It's a simple but profound structure and sequence.

Boy loved girl *and* the girl loved the boy, *but* their parents didn't agree with their relationship, *therefore* they decided to steal a car *and* run away together. *But* the car broke down, *therefore* they were forced to walk... (This could go on and on but I think you get the point.)

So you can see that conflict is a major factor in what makes a good story. But there are other potential factors at play.

A story is generally considered good when someone faces a problem which leads to change. An easy way to look at it is Character-Conflict-Change. Most literary works and Hollywood movies follow this well-worn path, and to great effect.

Joseph Campbell, a professor of literature, wrote a book called *The Hero with a Thousand Faces* in 1949. In that book he analyzed stories, myths, and fables from around the world and extracted a common pattern in the events and sequencing of these stories. He called this pattern the "monomyth." What he wrote set the template for almost every award-winning novel and blockbuster breakout movie you've ever seen.

It's known as the Hero's Journey. Essentially it has 3 parts: Departure, Initiation, and Return. But he originally had 17 different beats (acts) to describe the progression. I won't go through all 17 parts but I'll give you the broad strokes.

It follows how our hero moves from the common, ordinary world into the space of a special world outside of their comfort zone. It usually starts on an average day in an average place, doing an average activity.

Then there is an inciting incident. Perhaps someone has taken something away from the hero. Maybe they've taken someone they love, stolen their money, ruined their reputation, etc. The hero now faces conflict. Typically, the hero lacks confidence. They feel that they are not smart, fast, or powerful enough to overcome the enemy.

Enter the mentor. They meet someone who is often older, wiser, and more powerful than them in some way. The mentor will give them a tool or weapon to help, teach them special skills, or show them the power that they already have inside, but never realized.

The hero now enters the special world. The hero meets some like-minded allies but also some new enemies. While fighting some smaller battles, the hero realizes their strengths and weaknesses.

Finally, the hero faces their biggest challenge. It could be the big boss, a beast, the bad guy, or even their own personal fears or doubts. Usually the hero wins in the end, gets some reward, and lives to fight another day.

After the battle they return to the ordinary world with some prize or reward, but now they have changed – they have transformed!

This structure works and it's a tried-and-true, proven way to sequence a good story. But for business purposes, it's much too long and complicated. Also, not every story needs all the 17 beats.

So how can you structure your story to make sure it has all the right ingredients in the right order? There are many storytelling structures but I'll share the one I usually teach my clients. It's simple to understand, easy to remember, and the sequencing is built-in.

Enter the SHORT story formula. It works not only as a story structure, but a story structure that we can use for our entire presentation!
S = Situation
H = Hero
O = Obstacle
R = Resolution
T = Transformation

SITUATION (CONTEXT) - Where and when? What is happening right now? What just happened? What is about to happen? What are the mood and environment? How are people feeling? This gives the audience the background and helps them orient themselves and picture the scene as it was.

HERO (CHARACTER) - This doesn't necessarily mean superhero, it's just the main character – the protagonist. (This can be a person, team, company, client, product, or service.)

What do they want? What are their dreams and desires? What are their fears and frailties? What is their personality? What are their strengths and weaknesses? Who is their enemy?

OBSTACLE (CONFLICT) - What is the obstacle to the hero getting what they want? What will happen if they don't get it? Is the enemy a person, company, competition, situation, or even themselves (e.g. Limiting beliefs, procrastination, indecision, fear of failure, etc.)?

RESOLUTION (CONCLUSION) - How does the problem get solved? Does it get solved? What factors led to the story ending this way? What things did they try, yet didn't work? How do all the loose ends get resolved?

TRANSFORMATION (CHANGE) - This is the lessons learned, the moral of the story, the takeaway. How is the main CHARACTER different than in the beginning? How have they changed? How should that affect my personal and professional decisions?

Stories are all about CHANGE. We learn from stories and base our future decisions on past stories we have lived through and remember. When faced with a decision, your brain scans for similar precedents. Whether it comes up with negative or positive stories will strongly affect your viewpoint and thus your decision.

CONFLICT is what engages an audience. When we see the word "but" we automatically sense a problem. When we sense a problem, we automatically go into problem-solving mode.

Steve Jobs used this type of structure in his famous Stanford commencement speech. Now I never met him, but I could tell from his dealings with people, his book, and the movie that he wasn't always such a likable guy. So how does he start the speech in a way that will make him more likable? He starts off by being vulnerable and thus eliciting oxytocin.

"I never graduated from college. Truth be told, this is the closest I've ever gotten to a college graduation."

And just like that, he's set up his audience emotionally and he's off to the races.

"Today I want to tell you three stories from my life. That's it. No big deal. Just three stories."

This is my favorite line actually. The underselling, the under-promising he does here is amazing. Why do I say that?

Jobs believed in the power of storytelling. He once famously said that "the most powerful person in the world is the storyteller. The storyteller sets the vision, values, and agenda for an entire generation." Also, Jobs was the founder, chairman, and majority stakeholder of Pixar. Pixar is known as a storytelling company. And to top it all off, Jobs asked famed screenwriter Aaron Sorkin, best known for writing and directing the television series *The West Wing*, to help him with this speech!

So when Jobs says, "three stories...No big deal," please don't believe it for a second. Let's see how he did it.

SITUATION + HERO (CONTEXT + CHARACTER): In college, "I had no idea what I wanted to do with my life and no idea how college was going to help me figure it out. And here I was spending all of the money my parents had saved their entire life. So I decided to drop out..."

Here we know the time and place and he earlier gave details of his background, including events around his birth. We see a young Steve that is lost and aimless, hopelessly searching for a worthwhile purpose, while riddled with guilt over the money being poured on him.

OBSTACLE (CONFLICT): "Well, as Apple grew we hired someone who I thought was very talented to run the company with me, and for the first year or so things went well. But then our visions of the future began to diverge and eventually we had a falling out. When we did, our Board of Directors sided with him. So at 30 I was out. And very publicly out. What had been the focus of my entire adult life was gone, and it was devastating. I really didn't know what to do for a few months. I felt I had let the previous generation of entrepreneurs down – that I had dropped the baton as it was being passed to me."

We see the conflict of him working so hard, being so committed, and yet getting kicked out of his own company.

**RESOLUTION** (CONCLUSION): "But something slowly began to dawn on me – I still loved what I did. The turn of events at Apple had not changed that one bit. I had been rejected, but I was still in love. And so I decided to start over."

"During the next five years, I started a company named NeXT, another company named Pixar, and fell in love with an amazing woman who would become my wife. Pixar went on to create the world's first computer animated film, *Toy Story*, and is now the most successful animation studio in the world. In a remarkable turn of events, Apple bought NeXT, I returned to Apple, and the technology we developed at NeXT is at the heart of Apple's current renaissance."

Jobs here does some soul searching and decides to pick himself up, dust himself off, and carry on. His endeavors are successful and he returns to his former job at Apple.

**TRANSFORMATION** (CHANGE): "I'm pretty sure none of this would have happened if I hadn't been fired from Apple. It was awful tasting medicine, but I guess the patient needed it. Sometimes life hits you on the head with a brick. Don't lose faith. I'm convinced that's the only thing that kept me going was that I loved what I did. You've got to find what you love. And that is as true for your work as it is for your lovers. Your work is going to fill a large part of your life, and the only way to be truly satisfied is to do what you believe is great work. And the only way to do great work is to love what you do. If you have not found it yet, keep looking. Don't settle. As with all matters of the heart, you'll know when you find it. And like any great relationship, it just gets better and better as the years roll on. So keep looking until you find it. Don't settle."

We see that the hero here has changed from a lost and aimless youth to a decisive, driven, and determined man. He uses his stories to inspire and motivate the graduating students to find and follow their passions. The takeaway line being "Stay hungry, stay foolish." Brilliant!

When searching for your own stories, look for the conflict first. What situations have you faced that had conflict in them? A problem or a challenge? A villain or enemy? An obstacle or ordeal?

Once you've found that, share details about the context and background of the situation. Tell us who the main character is and what they want. When you tell us the conflict, make us feel the pain. Show us how it all ended and how all the loose ends worked out. And finally, help us to see how it should guide us in the future.

We can use the SHORT story formula for a story or anecdote within our presentation. But we can also use it as the structure for our entire presentation.

I sometimes get pushback from new clients on storytelling. One of the most common things they say is that their superiors don't want to hear stories. They say the second that they say they are going to tell a story, their bosses tell them not to, and to just tell the facts. So one quick point to share is that I never tell the audience I'm going to tell a story, I just tell it.

Many leaders have had to sit through tedious, boring, and downright manipulative stories, so they are often weary of stories.

Stories can be in the form of case studies or examples. Thinking of them this way alleviates any tension felt.

So another way to incorporate the principles of storytelling is to use the SHORT story framework as your presentation structure. A typical presentation structure is to start with a proposal and then to give supporting arguments and evidence for it afterwards. The SHORT storytelling structure is the opposite. It takes you on a journey as we go through the details in a step-by-step way.

For example, imagine that you are pitching or selling something to a potential client.

SITUATION - You set the scene by describing the current market, outlook, mood, and perhaps the offerings out there.

HERO - In this scenario your main character would be your potential client. Talk about who they are, what they are trying to do, and the things that concern and worry them. The more you can accurately describe their situation, the more they will feel that you understand them, and they will feel seen and acknowledged.

OBSTACLE - Show them that their current situation is undesirable and let them feel the heat. Sometimes your clients won't realize that they have a problem so you will need to help them open their eyes. Appealing to loss aversion can be an excellent way to help them to realize what they might lose if things go wrong.

RESOLUTION - If you've done your job of setting the scene, showing that you understand their goals and the extent of their problems, they should almost be asking you what to do next. Here is where you offer your solution to their problem. It can be your company, product, service, etc.

TRANSFORMATION - Here is where you paint a vivid picture of the future when their problem is solved and they have none of the worries and issues they have now. "Imagine never having to worry about...again!"

In this scenario, you didn't even have to tell a story. Instead you just used this same storytelling structure to share all your facts with them.

## Wooden Horses: Stealthy Stories

In my Strategic Storytelling workshops, I usually ask my participants if my name, Troy, evokes a famous story. If you're like them
you will probably think of the city of Troy and the epic story of the
Trojan horse. People welcomed the horse at face value, oblivious
to the hidden powerful elements within. Likewise, a strategic story
is readily accepted by your audience, yet has a hidden power
within.

Once we have gone through our
A|B|C methodology and specified
what we want our audiences to
think, feel, or do, we can tailor our
storytelling to attain that goal.

The easiest way to incorporate
storytelling into your presentations is to just think of a real
life example that proves the point
you are trying to make. But it's
important to understand the
main principle of storytelling – show, don't tell.

What does that mean? Think back to the chapter on CHANGES.
What is the perception that you want your audience to have of
you? It's easy to "tell" the audience that they can trust you, that
you are honest, and that you are competent. But why should they
believe you? In fact, often audiences react when they are told what
to think, feel, or do. They will often look for evidence that directly
opposes the presenter's direction.

Instead, why not subtly incorporate stories that "show" them that you are trustworthy, honest, and competent? Don't just "tell" them that you are trustworthy, "show" them through a story. Make them feel that you are trustworthy.

Of course, discernment and a subtle touch are needed. These mini-stories can be part of a larger story that we are telling. By adding and highlighting key qualities we want to show, we can gently help our audience grasp our hidden messages.

For example, in my Strategic Storytelling workshops, I have my participants go through the A|B|C methodology. When they get to CHANGE part and think about the way they want to be perceived, I ask them to write down a few words to describe themselves. I then ask them to think of a story that "shows" that quality in them. Then, without telling the rest of the class what the quality is, we listen to their story and try to guess afterwards what the quality is. Nine out of 10 times we can guess the quality correctly. Your audiences aren't looking for that in your stories but they will subconsciously pick up on it. The wooden horse has subtly done its work.

Don't just make vague promises that lack clarity for your audience. Sure, you can "tell" them that something is a bad idea and it's going to cause them a lot of trouble. But it's much better to "show" them the consequences by relaying a concrete example of someone who already went through that and painting a vivid picture of the pain it caused.

You can tell your audience that working with you will bring them success, freedom, and profits. How much better to show them what you have already done for others so that they can imagine themselves in that same scenario!

I come across many presentations in my work and a common thing I see is buzzwords and jargon that don't have a clear meaning or give the audience clear direction. Remember, one of the main tenets of business storytelling is "show, don't tell." Instead of defining something in rules, you can show your audience what something feels and looks like.

For example, Tony Hsieh was the CEO of Zappos, an online shoe store. Unfortunately he met an untimely passing just a few years ago. I always admired him for his clear goals and direction for his company.

But his most admirable quality was definitely his compassion for others. The company's motto was "Delivering happiness." Customer service was first and foremost. But just telling the staff that the customer comes first and you want them to be happy is rather vague and therefore open to interpretation.

How could he "show" them what he meant? He told the story of a woman who called to return a pair of men's slippers. When she was asked if there was something wrong with the slippers or delivery she said there were no problems and that everything was correct. She then told them  that they were for her husband, but he had unexpectedly passed away in a car crash before the shoes arrived.

The customer service staff extended their condolences and gave her an instant refund. After the call, she felt sad and told her workmates. They all decided to buy some flowers and sent them to her. She was so touched that she even mentioned this kind gesture at the funeral.

Tony explained that on a transactional basis, these types of inter-actions lose us both time and money. But for building a brand, for making a deep connection with the customer that leads to customer loyalty and word of mouth advertising, it was invaluable.

After hearing this story, his staff knew exactly what he meant by "Delivering happiness." They understood not only what he expect-ed of them but also what he was allowing and empowering them to do. A perfect example of show, don't tell.

Interestingly, he tells another, more upbeat, example of what he thought customer service should look like. He tells of how he was at a footwear conference with some fellow industry leaders from another company. After a long day at the conference, they all went back to the hotel room of one of the attendees for a nightcap. One woman kept talking about how hungry she was and her particular craving for a pepperoni pizza. Only problem was that it was late and room service was closed for the night. Not knowing the area, they had no idea if there was anything open near them.

Someone joked that they should call Zappos customer service since it's supposedly the best. The hungry woman took that liter-ally and actually called and put it on speakerphone. Tony didn't let his presence be known and the woman told the Zappos staff that she was craving a pepperoni pizza but room service was closed and she had heard that Zappos had the best customer service in the world. After a brief pause, the customer service rep said, "Hold on a minute, please." A minute later she came back with a list of the 5 names and numbers of pizza shops in that area that were still delivering. Now I don't know about you, but that's what I call customer service!

The best part about that story is not only that it shows compassionate customer service, and "Delivering happiness," but it reveals personality traits inherent at Zappos. The CEO is a guy you can have a few drinks with and share a late-night pizza together. Also, that he's confident enough to just sit back and trust that his staff will know how to handle the call respectfully. And that he has a good sense of humor as well. He never said these things, he showed them.

So look for opportunities to let the story make the greater point, instead of just spouting out overused expressions that are often open to interpretation and misunderstandings.

**Here's where the story ends.**

Storytelling is immensely powerful. Try to slowly incorporate stories into your presentations. Once you've mastered the SHORT story structure, you can experiment a bit and try the many other structures and templates out there.

Also, now that you learned about the 7 principles of persuasion, you can start to look for stories that appeal to those principles. More on that in my next book!

Another amazing effect of being in storytelling mode is that it usually calms the storyteller down. It's so natural for us to tell stories that we organically gesture and vary our vocals as we take on the differing situations and characters involved. Your presentations will be remembered and enjoyed, and your stealthy stories can be highly persuasive and convincing.

Your audience wants insights that will help them navigate this complex world. Yes, good strategic storytelling gives true meaning, insight, and clues to making future decisions based on past events. Stories have power. Be sure to harness these powerful BRIDGES in your next presentation!

Takeaways

- Use the SHORT formula to create memorable stories:

1. S=Situation (Context)

2. H= Hero (Character)

3. O=Obstacle (Conflict)

4. R=Resolution (Conclusion)

5. T=Transformation (Change)

- PHYSIOLOGICAL effects of storytelling involve dopamine, the reward and pleasure chemical; oxytocin, the love drug; serotonin, the good mood drug; endorphins, creating the stimulation of exhilaration; cortisol, the stress and anxiety hormone; and adrenaline, producing the fight, flight, or freeze feeling.

- PSYCHOLOGICAL effects include the Identifiable Victim Effect, the IKEA Effect, and the Zeigarnik Effect.

# THE LANDING

"Your problem is to bridge the gap which exists between where you are now and the goal you intend to reach."

Earl Nightingale

### The curious case of the caissons

W ORKING INSIDE THE WOODEN caissons was laborious and dangerous. For $2 a day, the sandhogs, as they were called, would dig inside the caisson towards the bedrock below.

Caissons used for the Bridge were large wooden airtight structures, first designed and used in Europe. They looked like an upside-down shoebox. But this shoebox was the size of a football field! They were built on land and floated to the spot where an underwater foundation was needed. The caisson was then deliberately sunk to the depths of the riverbed. An airtight elevator was attached, and the whole thing was pumped with air to make a pressurized, airtight working area.

In Brooklyn, this was used for removing layers of sand so that the caisson could eventually rest on bedrock, deep beneath the water. The work was work was dirty, difficult, and dangerous. Because the caissons were made of wood, leaks and floods were common. In addition to that, they were often lit by torches and oil lamps as electric lighting was relatively new and not suited for underwater use. Fires were a common danger as well.

Progress was slow and usually only achieved a few inches of depth a day. This is truly  amazing, considering the caisson's immense size. The working conditions were claustrophobic, suffocating, and humid. Holes in the caisson or uneven surfaces underneath caused the frequent leaks and flooding.

The air was damp and musty. And it was compressed air that was being pumped down into the caisson to keep air pressure high so that no water would leak in. This made breathing uneasy. It was hard to work for long hours.

"Inside the caisson, everything wore an unreal, weird appearance. There was a confused sensation in the head, like the rush of many waters. The pulse was at first accelerated, then sometimes fell below the normal rate. The voice sounded faint, unnatural, and it became a great effort to speak. What with the flaming lights, the deep shadows, the confusing noise of hammers, drills and chains, the half-naked forms flitting about, if of a poetic temperament, get a realizing sense of Dante's inferno. One thing to me was noticeable, time passed quickly in the caisson."– E.F. Farrington, master mechanic for Washington Roebling

There was also the ever-present threat of fires. Electric lighting was a relatively new invention and not safe enough at the time for underwater use. Therefore torches were used to light their work. Having torches near the wooden caissons meant that catching fire was a constant fear and occasional actuality.

On one such occasion, in 1870, Washington Roebling ventured deep down into the caisson to help put out the flames that could spell the end of the project and many lives as well. After a grueling fight with the flames in the suffocating close proximity of the caisson, he had to be surfaced quickly and carried home to be treated for his exhaustion.

Almost instantly after emerging, he felt unwell. Sharp pains coursed through his body, and strange sensations flashed here and there. That night he writhed in pain in a cold sweat. The caisson sickness was upon him.

The doctors rubbed his body with whiskey and salt. They believed that this would serve to aid his circulation. A strong-minded man, he returned the very next day to continue fighting the raging fire. All the while, he was in agony and pain.

Washington lay in his bed shivering with fever. It had been months since he fought that caisson fire. His body was riddled with pain, and where there was no pain, there was paralysis. His caring wife, Emily, sat at his side, trying to soothe the pains that ailed him.

What was being called Caissons Disease had reduced him to a pile of skin and bones.

Many theorized that the disease was caused by a mysterious gas that was only present in the depths of the riverbed and unearthed by the workers. This disease didn't only affect the daily laborers, though. It would continue to ravage the life of the chief engineer, Washington Roebling, and leave him blind, mute, debilitated, and half paralyzed. The cause would later be found to be something no one could have anticipated.

Washington Roebling died years later, never knowing the assailant that had struck him. It was to be many years later that science came to understand something we now call decompression sickness – the bends. The bends is a medical condition caused by the emergence of dissolved gases forming bubbles inside body tissue during decompression. This is common for scuba divers when they come up too quickly without proper depressurization.

It was impossible for the doctors to know about this at the time. A time when whiskey and salt were considered therapy.

B ABY'S GOT THE BENDS

Likewise, it's impossible to know exactly what our audiences think or feel. Often we are just guessing at what the barriers for them might be. We can do both demographics and psychographics and still not imagine why someone might not agree with our idea or want to change. Humans are complicated, and there are many things that we can't know about someone just from observations.

Sometimes it may be obvious with just a little observation, research, and discernment. Other times it may require using the process of elimination until we are left with something deeper, more psychological.

It's impossible to know what has shaped the personalities and psyches of people we work with and come across in business. We can only observe, guess, experiment, and then adapt.

Sometimes the process of elimination leads us to the real core issues that create a barrier for our audiences.

Observation and discernment are needed. Empathy is the ultimate skill here as it guides us through the process of elimination.

Yet, for most situations, a little due diligence, including research, questioning, and probing, can go a long way. It takes persistence and focus to find the BRIDGES as well.

There is a plaque on the Brooklyn Bridge mentioning the giant contribution of Emily Roebling. It reads...

THE BUILDERS OF THE BRIDGE DEDICATED TO THE MEM-
ORY OF
EMILY WARREN ROEBLING 1843 - 1903
WHOSE FAITH AND COURAGE HELPED HER STRICKEN
HUSBAND
COL. WASHINGTON A. ROEBLING, C.E. 1837 - 1926
COMPLETE THE CONSTRUCTION OF THIS BRIDGE FROM
THE PLANS OF HIS FATHER JOHN A. ROEBLING, C.E. 1805 -
1869 WHO GAVE HIS LIFE TO THE BRIDGE
BACK OF EVERY GREAT WORK WE CAN FIND
THE SELF-SACRIFICING DEVOTION OF A WOMAN

It's right there in plain sight, but not many see it, know the story, or understand the depths of truth it bears.

The Bridge still holds some other secrets, as well. Few know that there is a plaque mounted inside the anchorage on the Brooklyn side that covers a buried time capsule. The time capsule and its contents won't be revealed until May 24, 2083, which will mark the bicentennial of the bridge's completion. That may be beyond our lifetime.

But in this book, I sought to hold nothing back. I shared all the secrets I know to help you to give the most persuasive presentations imaginable. I shared with you all the psychological secrets I could cram in to this book of how people make decisions. More importantly, I gave practical applications of the principles and real world case studies and examples. You now know how to optimize your success rate by adding principled persuasion and influence in your presentations!

Let's do a quick review...

**AUDIENCE - BARRIERS + BRIDGES - CHANGE**

CHANGE
Purpose: What do I want my audience to think, feel, or do?

Perception: How do I want to be perceived? Or even more importantly, how does my audience need to perceive me to cross over to CHANGE?

AUDIENCE
Demographics: What is my audience? Male/female, rich/poor, old/young, local/foreign, etc.?

Psychographics: Who is my audience? What are their hobbies, passions, beliefs, personality, likes and dislikes? What makes them tick, and what ticks them off? What keeps them up at night, and what makes them get out of bed in the morning?

BARRIERS
Personal: What characteristics, unique to that individual, might make them resist CHANGE?

Professional: What factors common to everyone in this environment would prohibit or reduce your chances of moving your audience to CHANGE?

Physical: What tangible, visible, aesthetic factors might hinder your audience from making real CHANGE?

Psychological: What mental bias might be preventing your audience from processing your presentation the way that you desire?

Cognitive bias: Internal psychological filters that influence our judgments and decisions.

BRIDGES
PRINCIPLES OF PERSUASION- Tip the scales of persuasion to you with SCALES-U.

1/ SCARCITY- People value rare, unique, and fleeting things.
2/ CONSISTENCY AND COMMITMENT- People want to live up to their word and keep their promises.
3/ AUTHORITY- People tend to follow the lead and advice of experts.
4/ LIKING- People will collaborate and cooperate with people they like.
5/ EXCHANGE (RECIPROCITY)- People feel an obligation to pay back when something is given to them.
6/ SOCIAL PROOF (CONSENSUS)- People tend to follow the actions of others who are very similar to them.
7/ UNITY- People tend to favor and follow others that are an in-group that they identify with or one of their tribe.

STORYTELLING- The SHORT Story formula

Situation (Context) - Who, what, where, why, when?
Hero (Character) - Personality, character, wants, and desires.
Obstacle (Conflict) - The problem, the enemy.
Resolution (Conclusion) - How was the problem solved or why wasn't it solved?
Transformation (Change) - How the situation is better or worse than in the beginning and what we can learn/take away from the story.

I believe I've shared enough methodology, strategy, and psychology for you to implement into your presentations for years to come. Now your journey to more effective, impactful, and yes, truly persuasive presentations begins!

There is always more to be discovered in the field of persuasion and influence, and I will write more about it soon. For now, experiment and practice these core principles and skills, and I'll give you some more tips, tricks, and techniques in my next book.

# 人人都称赞帮自己过河的那座桥

**"Everyone praises the bridge that got them across."**

**Chinese proverb**

My hope is that this book serves as a BRIDGE for you!

All the best on your journey of persuasion and please reach out to tell me how this book has helped you or to see if I can help you or your organization directly!

Please visit my website: PresentationPersuasion.com

And feel free to write me at : Troy@presentationpersuasion.com

# REFERENCES +
# BIBLIOGRAPHY

## THE APROACH

Levitt, Steven D., and Stephen J. Dubner. (2006.) *Freakonomics*. New York: Harper Trophy.
Ariely, D. (2009.) *Predictably Irrational*. New York: HarperCollins.
Thaler, Richard H., and Cass R. Sunstein. (2009.) *Nudge*. New York: Penguin.
"There's a Fly in My Urinal"
https://www.verywellmind.com/phineas-gage-2795244
https://www.simplypsychology.org/phineas-gage.html
https://hbr.org/2006/01/decisions-and-desire
https://www.pwc.com/gx/en/issues/data-and-analytics/big-decisions-survey/assets/big-decisions2014.pdf
Aristotle. *The Rhetoric of Aristotle: a Translation*. (1909.) Cambridge: University Press.

## CHAPTER 1
McCullough, D. (2012.) *The Great Bridge: The epic story of the building of the Brooklyn bridge*. New York: Simon & Schuster.

## CHAPTER 2
https://www.psychologicalscience.org/publications/observer/obsonline/cambridge-analytica-story-casts-spotlight-on-psychographics.html
https://www.gsb.stanford.edu/insights/science-behind-cambridge-analytica-does-psychological-profiling-work
https://nardwuar.com/
https://www.esquire.com/entertainment/tv/a35991892/sean-evans-hot-ones-snl-skit-interview/
https://www.bbc.com/news/technology-49508091
https://www.entrepreneur.com/leadership/how-jack-ma-overcame-his-7-biggest-failures/275969
https://www.businessinsider.com/guides/learning/chris-voss-masterclass-review
Raz, T., and Voss, C. (2016.) *Never Split the Difference: Negotiating As If Your Life Depended on It*. New York: Harper Business.

## CHAPTER 3

https://www.verywellmind.com/prevalence-of-pho-bias-in-the-united-states-2671912
https://www.caranddriver.com/features/a35170274/gephyropho-bia-fear-of-bridges/
https://www.verywellmind.com/glossophobia-2671860
https://www.verywellmind.com/tips-for-managing-public-speak-ing-anxiety-3024336
https://www.sciencedirect.com/topics/neuroscience/cogni-tive-bias
https://hbr.org/2006/12/the-curse-of-knowledge

## CHAPTER 4

Davis, D. (2000.) *Klan-destine Relationships: A Black Man's Odyssey in the Ku Klux Klan.* London: VISION Paperbacks.
Loftus E.F., and Palmer, J. C. (1974.) "Reconstruction of automo-bile destruction: An example of the interaction between language and memory." *Journal of Verbal Learning and Verbal Behavior*, 13(5), 585–589. Mayer, R.E. (Ed.).
https://www.researchgate.net/publication/280925440_Measur-ing_Effects_of_Metaphor_in_a_Dynamic_Opinion_Landscape
https://www.psychologytoday.com/us/blog/neuronarra-tive/201105/whether-beast-or-virus-metaphor-is-powerful-stuff
https://behavioralscientist.org/5-studies-the-ubiqui-ty-of-metaphor/
https://www.nationalgeographic.com/science/arti-cle/is-crime-a-virus-or-a-beast-how-metaphors-shape-our-thoughts-and-decisions
https://harvardlawreview.org/2015/04/law-enforcements-war-rior-problem/
Bargh, J. (2018.) *Before You Know It: The Unconscious Reasons We Do What We Do.* New York: Windmill Books.
https://www.frontiersin.org/articles/10.3389/fp-syg.2021.584689/full
https://www.researchgate.net/publication/336652968_Form-ing_Impressions_of_Personality_A_Replica-tion_of_Asch's_1946_Evidence_for_a_Primacy-of-Warmth_Ef-

fect_in_Impression_Formation
https://www.imdb.com/title/tt1909348/
Duarte, N. (2013.) *Resonate: Present Visual Stories that Transform Audiences.* New York: John Wiley & Sons.
https://www.ted.com/talks/nancy_duarte_the_secret_structure_of_great_talks
https://b2bdecisionlabs.com/research-center/research-brief-whiteboard-vs-powerpoint/

## CHAPTER 5
Cialdini, Robert B. (2008.) *Influence.* 5th ed. Upper Saddle River, NJ: Pearson.
Kahneman, D., and Tversky, A. (1979.) "Prospect theory: An analysis of decision under risk." *Econometrica*, 47, 263-291.
https://www.sciencedirect.com/science/article/abs/pii/S0167811610000182
https://youtu.be/iG9CE55wbtY
https://youtu.be/xh1ROLEDyP4
https://en.wikipedia.org/wiki/Portal:Comedy/Selected_quote/17
https://www.inc.com/jeff-haden/how-to-use-franklin-effect-to-repair-build-stronger-bonds.html

## CHAPTER 6
https://uk.linkedin.com/posts/rorysutherland_advertising-communications-bevioural science-activity-6965937619817926657-KMfn
https://www.forbes.com/sites/tracybrower/2020/02/16/successful-change-management-6-surprising-reasons-people-resist-change-and-how-to-motivate-them-to-embrace-it-instead/
https://www.psychologistworld.com/memory/zeigarnik-effect-interruptions-memory

# ACKNOWLEDGEMENTS

**CONTRIBUTORS PAGE**

The following have helped me in a variety of ways: as inspiration, sounding boards, beta readers, moral supports, and everything in between.

**Inspirations, Revelations + Collaborations**
Jeremy Connell-Waite
Nancy Duarte
Rory Sutherland
Sam Tatam
David JP Phillips
Jonah Berger
Dan Ariely
Robert Cialdini
Steve Martin
Brian Ahearn
Zoe Chance
Daniel Pink
Matt Abrahams
Chris Do
Pete Judo
Akash Karia
Bri Williams
Louise Ward
Simon Lancaster
Dan and Chip Heath
Tiffany Tivasuradej
Liam Callaghan

**Motivation + Appreciation**
Cindy Pforte
Galen Callaghan
Jordan Hudson
Lindsay Prater
Mark Schold
Jamie Dixon

**Participation + Perspiration**
Bethany Marchesano
Denis Hiezely
David Pullan
Deepti Thomas
Emilia Zainel
Angel Hakker
Declan Foster
Renaud Taburiaux
Marcia Abramson
Fergal Kelly
Keith Hutchings
Nathan Musson
Truet Black
Tika Tika
Romana Baia
Andres Oliveros
Justin Yang
Catherine Leung
Cathy Han


*Photography, Illustrations, and typography by Troy Andrews
*Brooklyn Bridge architectural blueprint rendering by Bethany
Marchesano

"You'll miss her most when you roam,

'cause you'll think of her and think of home,

the good old Brooklyn Bridge."

**Frank Sinatra**

This book is dedicated to my father, **Wim 1935-2021,**

my mother, **Corinne** and my sister **Cindy.**

# ABOUT AUTHOR

Website: PresentationPersuasion.com

Hi, I'm Troy Andrews. I'm an executive presentation coach currently based in Asia.

I teach presentation design and delivery to business executives from such companies as Nike, Under Armour, Porsche, VW, HSBC, Mondelez, Rakuten, Cargill, Lindberg, Synopsys, and Splunk, just to name a few.

I've also taught and run workshops at institutions and organizations like Duke University, Jiaotong University, Fudan University School of Business, and the American Chamber of Commerce.

I focus on the persuasive + influential aspects of presentation design and delivery. I apply the principles of Behavioral Economics, Behavioral Science, and Persuasion Theory to business presentations.

I run a company called PresentationPersuasion.com. I facilitate group workshops as well as individual executive presentation coaching. Check out the site to see what I'm up to, connect, and explore ways we can collaborate!

Write me at: Troy@presentationpersuasion.com

Also, if you liked the book, please leave a review on Goodreads, Amazon, or wherever you purchased the book. It would mean so much to me!

www.ingramcontent.com/pod-product-compliance
Lightning Source LLC
Chambersburg PA
CBHW020244290326
41930CB00038B/259